1000 FACTS ABOUT THE UNITED STATES OF AMERICA VOL. 1

Contents

Introduction 6

Alabama 7

Alaska 9

Arizona 11

Arkansas 13

California 15

Colorado 17

Connecticut 19

Delaware 21

Florida 23

Georgia 25

Hawaii 27

Idaho 29

Illinois 31

Indiana 33

Iowa 35

Kansas 37

Kentucky 39

Louisiana 41

Maine 43

Maryland 45

Massachusetts..47

Michigan...49

Minnesota...51

Mississippi..53

Missouri..55

Montana..57

Nebraska...59

Nevada...61

New Hampshire...63

New Jersey..65

New Mexico..67

New York..69

North Carolina..71

North Dakota..73

Ohio...75

Oklahoma...77

Oregon...79

Pennsylvania..81

Rhode Island..83

South Carolina...85

South Dakota...87

Tennessee..89

Texas...91

Utah 93

Vermont 95

Virginia 97

Washington 99

West Virginia 101

Wisconsin 103

Wyoming 105

Conclusion 107

"America is too great for small dreams."

— Ronald Reagan

Introduction

Welcome to the first volume of "1000 Facts about The United States of America," an enlightening journey across the vast landscapes of one of the world's most diverse and intriguing countries. This volume, the first of three, invites you to embark on an exciting adventure, exploring the unique qualities that define the United States through a series of fascinating facts about its states.

From the shimmering shores of the Atlantic to the rugged peaks of the Pacific coast, each state in this great nation boasts a distinctive blend of history, culture, and natural beauty. Each fact, carefully curated and succinctly presented, illuminates a different facet of American life, drawing a vibrant mosaic of the country's collective identity.

In this volume, we delve into an eclectic array of information spanning historical milestones, cultural oddities, significant landmarks, natural wonders, economic marvels, and so much more. We strive to present a comprehensive picture, depicting the essence of America in all its complexities, contradictions, and charms.

Whether you're an American citizen seeking to discover more about your home country, or a curious globe-trotter with an interest in the breadth of U.S. culture, this collection of facts provides an accessible, engaging, and thoroughly enjoyable route to understanding the United States. Let's journey together through the pages, unearthing the treasures buried in the rich soils of America, one state at a time. Embrace the exploration, and let your discovery of the United States begin with "1000 Facts about The United States of America vol. 1".

Daniel Scott

Alabama

- **Founding Father:** Alabama became the 22nd state of the United States on December 14, 1819.
- **Meteorological Marvel:** Alabama is home to the only temperate rainforest in the lower 48 states, the Sipsey Wilderness.
- **Railway Innovation:** Alabama was the first state to build a railroad specifically for carrying coal in 1831.
- **Musical Roots:** The legendary Muscle Shoals Sound Studio in Alabama helped shape the careers of iconic musicians like Aretha Franklin and the Rolling Stones.
- **Space Race:** Huntsville, Alabama, is known as the Rocket City because it's where the Saturn V rocket was built, the rocket that sent humans to the moon.
- **Boll Weevil Monument:** Enterprise, Alabama, is home to the only monument in the world honoring an insect, the boll weevil, which changed the region's agriculture from cotton to diversified crops.
- **Cultural Celebration:** Alabama hosts the oldest Mardi Gras celebration in the United States, predating New Orleans by over a decade.
- **Landmark Ruling:** The 1955 Montgomery Bus Boycott in Alabama led to the U.S. Supreme Court ruling that segregation on public buses was unconstitutional.
- **Automotive Powerhouse:** Alabama is one of the leading states in the U.S. in auto manufacturing, with factories from Mercedes-Benz, Honda, and Hyundai.
- **Famed Inventor:** Alabama native George Washington Carver developed over 300 products using peanuts, contributing significantly to the agricultural and economic prosperity of the South.
- **Literary Legend:** Alabama is the birthplace of iconic "To Kill a Mockingbird" author, Harper Lee.

- **Highest Point:** Cheaha Mountain, Alabama's highest point, reaches 2,407 feet above sea level.
- **Diverse Ecosystems:** Alabama has one of the highest levels of biodiversity in the United States, including 77,000 miles of rivers and streams.
- **Deep-Sea Fishing:** Alabama is known as the Red Snapper capital of the world, thanks to its robust coastal fishing industry.
- **Football Frenzy:** The University of Alabama's football team, the Crimson Tide, has won numerous national championships.
- **Cave Exploration:** Alabama houses one of the highest concentrations of caves in the U.S, with over 4,000 recorded caves.
- **Cotton State:** Alabama was once the top cotton producer in the U.S. during the 19th century.
- **Rosa Parks:** The Civil Rights Movement was sparked in Montgomery, Alabama, when Rosa Parks refused to give up her seat on a city bus.
- **Helen Keller:** The first deaf-blind person to earn a Bachelor of Arts degree, Helen Keller, was born in Tuscumbia, Alabama.
- **Biodiversity Hotspot:** Alabama ranks fifth in the nation for overall species diversity and is first among states east of the Mississippi River.

Alaska

- **Last Frontier:** Alaska was purchased from Russia in 1867 and became the 49th state of the United States in 1959.
- **Tallest Peak:** Denali, the highest peak in North America, is located in Alaska, standing at 20,310 feet.
- **Wilderness Abundance:** Alaska has more national park land than all other states combined, with over 54 million acres.
- **Longest Coastline:** Alaska boasts the longest coastline of all U.S. states, at more than 34,000 miles.
- **Aurora Borealis:** Fairbanks, Alaska, is one of the best places in the world to see the Northern Lights.
- **Permanent Fund Dividend:** Since 1982, Alaskan residents have received an annual payment, the Permanent Fund Dividend, from investment earnings of mineral royalties.
- **Furry Friends:** Dog mushing is the official state sport of Alaska, celebrated annually in the 1,000-mile Iditarod Trail Sled Dog Race.
- **Sunlight Surplus:** Barrow, the northernmost city in the U.S., experiences over 80 days of continuous sunlight every summer.
- **Iditarod Trail:** The Iditarod Trail Sled Dog Race, running over 1,100 miles from Anchorage to Nome, is one of the world's top long-distance sled dog races.
- **Bear Paradise:** Alaska is home to the highest concentration of brown bears in the world, with an estimated population of 32,000.
- **Gold Rush History:** The 1896 discovery of gold in the Yukon led to the Klondike Gold Rush, greatly impacting Alaska's development.
- **Pipeline Engineering:** The Trans-Alaska Pipeline spans 800 miles, moving oil from the Arctic to the Gulf of Alaska.
- **Native Cultures:** Alaska has a rich Native heritage, with over 200 federally recognized tribes.

- **Glacial Wonders:** Alaska has an estimated 100,000 glaciers, covering 5% of the state.
- **Largest State:** Alaska is the largest state in the U.S. by land area, more than twice the size of Texas.
- **No Counties:** Unlike other states, Alaska does not have counties but is divided into 20 "boroughs."
- **Active Volcanoes:** Alaska is home to 80% of all active volcanoes in the U.S.
- **Fishing Industry:** Alaska's commercial fishing industry catches more seafood—over 6 billion pounds annually—than all the other states combined.
- **Eagle Gathering:** The Chilkat Bald Eagle Preserve in Haines, Alaska, hosts one of the world's largest gatherings of bald eagles annually.
- **Record Temperature:** Alaska holds the record for the lowest temperature in the U.S.: -80 degrees Fahrenheit in Prospect Creek.

Arizona

- **Grand Canyon:** Arizona is home to the Grand Canyon, one of the Seven Natural Wonders of the World.
- **Meteor Crater:** The best-preserved meteorite impact site on Earth, Meteor Crater, is located in Arizona.
- **Desert State:** Arizona is home to the Sonoran Desert, the hottest desert in Mexico and the United States.
- **London Bridge:** The original London Bridge was shipped stone-by-stone and reconstructed in Lake Havasu City, Arizona.
- **Saguaro National Park:** The park is home to the nation's largest cacti, the giant saguaro, a symbol of the American West.
- **Navajo Nation:** Arizona is home to the largest Native American reservation in the U.S., the Navajo Nation.
- **Copper Production:** Arizona leads the nation in copper production; it's even nicknamed the Copper State.
- **Sunniest City:** Yuma, Arizona, is the sunniest place on Earth, according to Guinness World Records.
- **State Gun:** Arizona has an official state gun, the Colt Single Action Army revolver.
- **Arizona Cardinals:** The Cardinals, originally from Chicago, are the oldest continuously run professional football team in the nation.
- **Bola Tie:** The official state neckwear of Arizona is the bola tie.
- **Petrified Forest:** Arizona's Petrified Forest National Park contains one of the largest and most colorful concentrations of petrified wood in the world.
- **Four Corners:** Arizona is one of the four U.S. states (Arizona, Colorado, New Mexico, and Utah) that meet at a common point.
- **Largest Pueblo:** The Hopi village of Oraibi is the oldest Native American settlement in the U.S.
- **O.K. Corral:** The legendary 30-second gunfight at the O.K. Corral took place in Tombstone, Arizona.

- **Roadrunner Tradition:** According to local legend, the roadrunner was god's dog to the Pima and Maricopa tribes in Arizona.
- **Hover Dam:** Arizona shares the Hoover Dam, one of the greatest engineering projects in history, with Nevada.
- **Low Precipitation:** Phoenix, Arizona, receives less rainfall annually than any other major city in the U.S.
- **Gadsden Purchase:** Southern Arizona was acquired from Mexico in the Gadsden Purchase of 1853.
- **Rattlesnake Haven:** Arizona has 13 species of rattlesnakes, more than any other state.

Arkansas

- **Hot Springs National Park:** Known as "The American Spa," this park around the city of Hot Springs was America's first federally protected area.
- **World's Only Diamond Mine:** Crater of Diamonds State Park is the only diamond mine in the world where you can keep what you find.
- **Bauxite Mining:** Arkansas was once the world's largest producer of bauxite, the ore from which aluminum is made.
- **Headquarters of Walmart:** The global retail giant was founded in Bentonville, Arkansas, where its headquarters still remain.
- **Toothbrush Capital:** The city of Jonesboro manufactures more toothbrushes than any other city in the U.S.
- **Clinton Presidential Library:** Arkansas is the birthplace and home of the 42nd President, Bill Clinton, and the site of his Presidential Library.
- **State Nickname:** Known as "The Natural State" due to its diverse landscapes from mountains to river valleys, dense woodland to fertile plains.
- **Magnet Cove:** A small city in Arkansas that has over 100 varieties of minerals within its boundaries.
- **Famous Musicians:** Johnny Cash and Glen Campbell were born in Arkansas, contributing significantly to country music.
- **First Woman Senator:** Hattie Caraway, the first woman elected to the United States Senate, was from Arkansas.
- **State Bird:** The mockingbird, known for its intelligence and ability to mimic the sounds of other birds, is the state bird of Arkansas.
- **State Gem:** Arkansas adopted the diamond as its official state gem in 1967 due to the diamond mine in Murfreesboro.
- **Arkansas Post:** The first European settlement in the lower Mississippi Valley, established by French explorers in 1686.

- **Tyson Foods:** The world's largest processor and marketer of chicken, beef, and pork is based in Springdale, Arkansas.
- **Mammoth Spring:** One of the world's largest springs flows nine million gallons of water hourly, forming a scenic 10-acre lake.
- **Mississippi River:** Arkansas is bordered by the Mississippi River, one of the longest rivers in the world.
- **Fruit Bowl:** Johnson County in Arkansas is known as the "Peach Capital" of the state, and the Altus area is recognized as the state's wine capital.
- **Gillett Coon Supper:** Gillett, Arkansas, is famous for its annual "Coon Supper," a raccoon-centric feast held to raise money for local scholarships.
- **Toltec Mounds:** These mounds are the remains of the ceremonial and governmental complex of an ancient Native American civilization.
- **First Woman Governor:** Arkansas was the third state to elect a woman as governor: Ella T. Grasso in 1975.

California

- **Silicon Valley:** California is home to the world's tech giants, including Google, Apple, anc Facebook, in a region known as Silicon Valley.
- **Hollywood:** Known as the entertainment capital of the world, it's home to the stars and birthplace of American cinema.
- **Golden Gate Bridge:** An engineering marvel and one of the most photographed bridges in the world, it spans the Golden Gate Strait.
- **Sequoia National Park:** The world's largest tree, General Sherman, stands in this national park, highlighting the state's natural grandeur.
- **Death Valley:** The hottest, driest, and lowest national park, it's a land of extremes and home to diverse desert wildlife.
- **California Gold Rush:** The discovery of gold in 1848 led to the largest mass migration in U.S. history, changing the state's demographics dramatically.
- **Diverse Ecosystem:** From coastal to desert, alpine to fertile valley, California is home to diverse ecosystems and rich biodiversity.
- **Largest State Economy:** If California were a country, it would have the 5th largest economy in the world.
- **Cesar Chavez:** Known for his role in labor rights, Chavez was a leader in California's farm labor movement.
- **Yosemite National Park:** Known for its waterfalls, deep valleys, grand meadows, and ancient giant sequoias, Yosemite is a national treasure.
- **Wine Production:** California produces more than 80% of all U.S. wine and is the world's 4th largest wine producer.
- **California Cuisine:** Known for a unique culinary style that highlights fresh, locally sourced ingredients and a fusion of various food cultures.

- **Pacific Crest Trail:** This 2,650-mile long trail, providing breathtaking scenic beauty, runs through California from Mexico to Canada.
- **Fortune Cookie Invention:** The modern version of the fortune cookie was invented by Makoto Hagiwara in San Francisco.
- **Oldest Public University:** The University of California system, founded in 1868, is one of the oldest public university systems in the U.S.
- **Tallest Living Things:** The coastal redwoods in California are the tallest living trees and things on Earth.
- **The Oscars:** The Academy Awards, also known as the Oscars, are held annually in Hollywood, celebrating excellence in cinematic achievements.
- **Disneyland:** Opened in 1955, Disneyland, located in Anaheim, is one of the most visited tourist destinations worldwide.
- **State Flower:** The California Poppy, with its bright orange blooms, is the state's official flower.
- **Mount Whitney:** The highest summit in the contiguous United States, it towers 14,494 feet above sea level.

Colorado

- **Pikes Peak:** Also known as America's Mountain, this peak inspired the lyrics for the song "America the Beautiful."
- **Colorado River:** Originating from the Rocky Mountains, it's one of the principal rivers of the Southwestern U.S and northern Mexico.
- **Denver Broncos:** One of the NFL's most successful teams, they've won multiple Super Bowls and have a large, passionate fan base.
- **Rocky Mountain National Park:** Famous for its stunning mountain views, alpine wildflowers, and abundant wildlife, including elk and bighorn sheep.
- **Legalization of Cannabis:** In 2012, Colorado became the first state to legalize cannabis for recreational use.
- **Four Corners Monument:** The only place in the U.S. where you can stand in four states at once: Colorado, New Mexico, Arizona, and Utah.
- **Aspen's Ski Resorts:** Known for its world-class ski resorts and the rich and famous who frequent them.
- **Cheyenne Mountain Zoo:** America's only mountain zoo, home to over 900 animals and situated at an elevation of 6,800 feet.
- **U.S. Air Force Academy:** Located in Colorado Springs, it's an undergraduate college for officer candidates for the United States Air Force.
- **Denver Mint:** Producing more than 50 million coins a day, it's one of the two U.S. mints where coins are produced for circulation.
- **Craft Beer Capital:** Colorado has the highest number of craft breweries per capita in the U.S.
- **Denver International Airport:** Known for its iconic peaked roof, it's the largest airport by total land area in the U.S.

- **Royal Gorge Bridge:** One of the world's highest suspension bridges, it spans the Arkansas River at a height of 955 feet.
- **Colorado Springs:** Home to Pikes Peak and the Garden of the Gods, it's a haven for outdoor enthusiasts.
- **Great Sand Dunes National Park:** Home to the tallest sand dunes in North America, with a maximum height of 750 feet.
- **Red Rocks Amphitheatre:** A unique open-air amphitheatre built into a rock structure near Morrison, offering stunning views and acoustics.
- **Leadville:** The highest incorporated city in the U.S., located at an elevation of 10,152 feet.
- **Dinosaur National Monument:** Shared with Utah, it's famous for its dinosaur fossils and petroglyphs.
- **Ute Tribe:** The indigenous Ute people, for whom the state is named, have lived in the region for centuries.
- **Colorado Ballet:** Founded in 1951, it's now one of the state's oldest and most successful arts institutions.

Connecticut

- **The Constitution State:** Connecticut got its nickname for the "Fundamental Orders," which is considered one of the first constitutions in history.
- **Yale University:** Founded in 1701, it's the third-oldest institution of higher education in the United States.
- **First Hamburger:** Louis' Lunch in New Haven claims to have served the first hamburger in the U.S. back in 1900.
- **Mystic Seaport:** The largest maritime museum in the U.S., it offers a look into New England's seafaring past with its historic ships and exhibits.
- **Mark Twain House:** Located in Hartford, it's where the famous author wrote his most well-known works, including "Adventures of Huckleberry Finn."
- **Gillette Castle State Park:** The eccentric home of actor William Gillette, designed to resemble a medieval castle, is now a public park.
- **Connecticut River:** The longest river in New England, it flows through four states from the Canadian border to Long Island Sound.
- **Connecticut's Coastline:** Despite being one of the smallest states, Connecticut has a shoreline that stretches for 332 miles.
- **Peabody Museum of Natural History:** Located at Yale University, it's famous for its Great Hall of Dinosaurs.
- **Lake Compounce:** Opened in 1846, it's the oldest continuously operating amusement park in the U.S.
- **First Helicopter Flight:** In 1939, the first practical helicopter took off in Stratford, thanks to pioneering engineer Igor Sikorsky.
- **Wadsworth Atheneum:** Located in Hartford, it's the oldest continuously-operating public art museum in the U.S.
- **Submarine Capital of the World:** Groton is home to the U.S. Navy's primary East Coast submarine base.

- **Mystic Aquarium:** Home to thousands of species of marine life, including beluga whales, it's one of the premier aquariums in the U.S.
- **Scoville Memorial Library:** America's oldest publicly funded library, it has been lending books since 1771.
- **Hartford Courant:** Established in 1764, it's the oldest continuously published newspaper in the U.S.
- **Litchfield Law School:** Opened in 1784, it was the first law school in the U.S.
- **Merritt Parkway:** Known for its scenic beauty and distinctive bridges, it was designated as a National Scenic Byway in 1996.
- **First Frisbee:** The flying disc toy known as the Frisbee was first produced in Connecticut by the Wham-O company.
- **Danbury's Hat History:** Danbury was once the hat-making capital of the world, with over 50 hat factories in the 19th century.

Delaware

- **The First State:** Delaware was the first state to join the Union, ratifying the U.S. Constitution on December 7, 1787.
- **Dover International Speedway:** Known as the "Monster Mile," this NASCAR track is one of the sport's most challenging.
- **Delaware Memorial Bridge:** The world's second-longest twin suspension bridge, it's a major route on the Eastern Seaboard.
- **Delaware's Size:** Despite being the second smallest state in the U.S., Delaware is densely populated and highly industrialized.
- **Fort Delaware:** Located on Pea Patch Island, this Civil War fortress once held Confederate prisoners of war.
- **Du Pont Family:** This influential family founded the chemical company DuPont and built numerous grand estates throughout the state.
- **Hagley Museum and Library:** Located on the site of the original du Pont gunpowder mills, it explores the early days of American industry.
- **Winterthur Museum, Garden and Library:** Formerly a Du Pont family estate, it's now a premier museum of American decorative arts.
- **Tax-Free Shopping:** Delaware is one of only five states with no sales tax, making it a shopper's paradise.
- **Delaware Bay:** The estuary outlet of the Delaware River, it's one of the most important bird migration areas in North America.
- **John Dickinson House:** Also known as Poplar Hall, it was the boyhood home of a Founding Father and "Penman of the Revolution."
- **Mason-Dixon Line:** This famous boundary between the North and South runs along the western and southern border of Delaware.
- **Lewes:** The town of Lewes was the first European settlement in Delaware, founded by Dutch settlers in 1631.

- **Horseshoe Crabs:** Delaware Bay is the world's largest spawning ground for horseshoe crabs.
- **Nemours Mansion and Gardens:** Another Du Pont estate, this 300-acre park features a grand mansion and one of the largest French gardens in North America.
- **Rehoboth Beach:** Known as the "Nation's Summer Capital," it's a popular seaside resort with a vibrant boardwalk.
- **Wilmington Blue Rocks:** This Minor League Baseball team is known for its fun atmosphere and unique mascot, Rocky Bluewinkle.
- **The Green, Dover:** This historic square was the location of many rallies, troop reviews, and other patriotic events during the American Revolution.
- **Delaware Breakwater East End Lighthouse:** Built in 1885, it's an iconic symbol of Delaware's maritime heritage.
- **Bethany Beach:** A popular family-friendly seaside resort known for its clean beaches and charming boardwalk.

Florida

- **Sunshine State:** Florida is known as the "Sunshine State" due to its warm climate and abundant sunshine.
- **Disney World:** The most visited vacation resort in the world, located in Orlando, Florida.
- **Everglades National Park:** A U.S. National Park that protects the southern 20 percent of the original Everglades ecosystem.
- **Florida Keys:** A string of tropical islands stretching about 120 miles off the state's southern tip.
- **Miami's Art Deco Historic District:** Contains the world's largest collection of Art Deco architecture, with over 800 buildings.
- **Florida's Alligators:** Florida is home to an estimated 1.3 million alligators, found in all 67 counties.
- **Kennedy Space Center:** NASA's primary launch center for human spaceflight since 1968.
- **St. Augustine:** The oldest city in the U.S., founded by Spanish explorers in 1565.
- **Ernest Hemingway Home:** A landmark and museum in Key West that was the residence of author Ernest Hemingway.
- **Orlando's Theme Parks:** Besides Disney World, Orlando is home to Universal Orlando Resort, SeaWorld Orlando, and Legoland Florida.
- **Miami Beach:** Known for its iconic sandy beaches, pastel-colored buildings, and vibrant nightlife.
- **Cape Canaveral:** Known as the site of major space shuttle launches and home to the Air Force Space & Missile Museum.
- **Florida Orange Juice:** Florida produces more than 70% of the U.S.'s supply of citrus, most of it for orange juice.
- **Seven Mile Bridge:** One of the longest bridges in the world, located in the Florida Keys.
- **Biscayne National Park:** A U.S. National Park that preserves Biscayne Bay, one of the top scuba diving areas in the U.S.

- **Ponce de León's Fountain of Youth:** A mythical spring that supposedly restores the youth of anyone who drinks its waters, sought by Juan Ponce de León in Florida.
- **Dry Tortugas National Park:** A remote park about 70 miles west of Key West, known for Fort Jefferson and abundant sea life.
- **Florida Panthers:** An endangered subspecies of cougar that lives in the forests and swamps of southern Florida.
- **Florida Manatee:** These gentle marine mammals are an official state marine mammal and can be found in Florida's warm waters.
- **Lake Okeechobee:** The largest freshwater lake in Florida and the second-largest body of freshwater in the contiguous United States.

Georgia

- **Peach State:** Georgia is nicknamed the "Peach State" due to the abundance of peaches grown in the state.
- **Atlanta:** This city is the state capital, the most populous city in Georgia, and the primary transportation hub of the southeastern United States.
- **Stone Mountain:** A quartz monzonite dome monadnock, Stone Mountain is the site of a famous giant carving commemorating Confederate leaders.
- **Martin Luther King Jr.:** The civil rights leader was born in Atlanta in 1929.
- **Coca-Cola:** The world-renowned beverage was invented in Atlanta by pharmacist John Pemberton in 1886.
- **Savannah's Historic District:** One of the largest National Historic Landmark Districts in the United States.
- **Georgia Aquarium:** Located in Atlanta, it was the largest aquarium in the world from its opening in 2005 until 2012.
- **Peanut Production:** As of 2021, Georgia grows more peanuts than any other state.
- **Okefenokee Swamp:** One of the largest intact freshwater ecosystems in the world, located in Georgia's southeast corner.
- **Appalachian Trail:** The southern terminus of this 2,200-mile trail is in Georgia's Springer Mountain.
- **CNN Headquarters:** The Cable News Network was founded in Atlanta by media mogul Ted Turner in 1980.
- **University of Georgia:** Founded in 1785, it's one of the oldest public universities in the United States.
- **Golden Isles:** A group of barrier islands off the coast, known for their beautiful resorts and natural splendor.
- **Georgia's Pecans:** More than 100 commercial pecan varieties come from Georgia.

- **Vidalia Onions:** Known for their sweetness, they are grown exclusively in a defined region of Georgia.
- **Atlanta Braves:** The Major League Baseball franchise has called Atlanta home since 1966.
- **Tybee Island:** Known for its wide, sandy beaches, including South Beach, home to the Tybee Pier and Pavilion.
- **Fort Pulaski:** A key Civil War structure, notable for the Union's successful experimental use of rifled cannon.
- **The Masters Tournament:** An annual professional golf tournament played at Augusta National Golf Club.
- **Atlanta Hawks:** A professional basketball team and member of the Southeast Division of the Eastern Conference in the National Basketball Association.

Hawaii

- **Aloha State:** Hawaii is universally known as the "Aloha State," reflecting the warmth and friendliness of the local culture.
- **Island Chain:** Hawaii is composed of 137 islands spanning 1,500 miles, making it the longest island chain in the world.
- **Active Volcanoes:** It's home to two of the world's most active volcanoes, Kilauea and Mauna Loa.
- **Honolulu:** Hawaii's state capital is the most remote major city in the world.
- **Pearl Harbor:** The site of the December 7, 1941, attack by Japan which led to the U.S. entering World War II.
- **Mauna Kea:** This dormant volcano is the highest point in the state, and when measured from its oceanic base, it's the tallest mountain on Earth.
- **Hawaiian Language:** Alongside English, Hawaiian is an official language in the state, the only U.S. state with two official languages.
- **Surfing:** The sport was invented by the Polynesians who first settled the islands.
- **Iolani Palace:** Located in Honolulu, it's the only royal palace in the United States.
- **Nene Goose:** The nene is the official state bird and is endemic to the Hawaiian Islands.
- **Hula Dance:** This Polynesian dance form accompanied by chant or song is a significant cultural tradition in Hawaii.
- **Kamehameha Day:** Hawaii uniquely observes this state holiday in honor of King Kamehameha I, the monarch who established the unified Kingdom of Hawaii.
- **Rainbow State:** Hawaii is often referred to as the "Rainbow State" due to frequent rainbows caused by the tropical, rainy environment.

- **Hawaiian Monk Seal:** One of the most endangered seal species in the world is native to Hawaii.
- **Aloha Shirt:** Also known as the Hawaiian Shirt, this style of dress shirt originated in Hawaii in the early 20th century.
- **State Fish:** The state fish is the Humuhumunukunukuapua'a, also known as the reef triggerfish.
- **Kona Coffee:** Coffee from the Kona Districts is world-renowned for its distinctive, rich flavors.
- **Haleakala National Park:** The park on Maui includes the dormant Haleakala Volcano and protects the endangered Hawaiian goose.
- **Lava Tubes:** The state has extensive lava tube systems, some of which are open for tourist exploration.
- **Waikiki Beach:** This world-renowned tourist spot in Honolulu is known for its long rolling surf, ideal for boarding and swimming.

Idaho

- **Potato State:** Idaho produces about one-third of the potatoes grown in the United States, making it the nation's largest producer.
- **Gem State:** Idaho is known as the "Gem State" because nearly every known type of gemstone has been found here.
- **Sun Valley:** This resort city is recognized as "the birthplace of destination skiing."
- **Bird of Prey:** Idaho is home to the Peregrine Fund's World Center for Birds of Prey, which helped the Peregrine Falcon recover from near-extinction.
- **Hell's Canyon:** At 7,993 feet deep, Hell's Canyon is the deepest river gorge in North America.
- **State Dance:** Idaho's state dance is the square dance, a traditional folk dance with four couples arranged in a square.
- **City of Trees:** Boise, the state capital, is known as the "City of Trees."
- **Idaho Territory:** Abraham Lincoln established the Idaho Territory on March 4, 1863.
- **Atomic City:** The city of Arco was the first in the world to be lit by atomic power in 1955.
- **Shoshone Falls:** Often referred to as the "Niagara of the West," Shoshone Falls is actually higher than Niagara Falls.
- **Lake Pend Oreille:** Idaho's largest lake is also the fifth-deepest lake in the United States.
- **Silver Valley:** This area in the Idaho Panhandle was once the richest silver district in the world.
- **Idaho State Horse:** The Appaloosa, a horse breed known for its spotted coat, is the official state horse.
- **Basque Community:** Boise has one of the highest concentrations of Basque Americans in the United States.

- **White Pine:** The Western White Pine, the state tree, can grow over 150 feet tall.
- **Famous Potatoes:** Idaho's license plates bear the slogan "Famous Potatoes."
- **Boise River Greenbelt:** This "ribbon of green" stretches 25 miles along the Boise River, providing scenic paths for biking and hiking.
- **Ernest Hemingway:** The famed author lived in Sun Valley and is buried in Ketchum, Idaho.
- **Center of the Universe:** The town of Wallace declared itself the "Center of the Universe" in 2004.
- **Craters of the Moon:** This national monument and preserve features a vast ocean of lava flows, cinder cones, and sagebrush.

Illinois

- **Prairie State:** Illinois is often referred to as the "Prairie State," with vast areas once covered by prairie grasses.
- **Chicago:** The state's largest city, Chicago, is the third most populous city in the United States.
- **First Skyscraper:** Chicago was home to the world's first skyscraper, the Home Insurance Building, built in 1885.
- **Lincoln's Home:** Abraham Lincoln lived in Springfield, Illinois until he moved to the White House. His home is now a National Historic Site.
- **Route 66:** The historic Route 66 starts in Chicago, Illinois and travels all the way to Santa Monica, California.
- **Nuclear Power:** The world's first nuclear reaction took place at the University of Chicago in 1942 under the leadership of Enrico Fermi.
- **Mississippi River:** The western border of Illinois is delineated by the Mississippi River.
- **State Dance:** Illinois designated square dancing as the official state American Folk Dance in 1990.
- **Tallest Building:** The Willis Tower (formerly known as the Sears Tower) in Chicago was once the tallest building in the world.
- **Barack Obama:** Former U.S. President Barack Obama started his political career in Illinois as a state senator.
- **State Bird:** The Northern Cardinal, known for its bright red color and melodious song, is the state bird of Illinois.
- **Great Lakes:** Illinois has 63 miles of coastline along Lake Michigan, one of the five Great Lakes.
- **World's Fair:** The 1893 World's Columbian Exposition in Chicago introduced the world to the Ferris wheel.
- **State Capital:** The state capital, Springfield, is home to the Abraham Lincoln Presidential Library and Museum.

- **Navy Pier:** Chicago's Navy Pier is one of the most visited attractions in the Midwest, featuring a Ferris wheel, carousel, and other family-friendly activities.
- **Illinois River:** This major waterway provided a vital transportation route for Native Americans and early European explorers.
- **Deep Dish Pizza:** This style of pizza was invented in Chicago and has become famous worldwide.
- **John Deere:** The agricultural machinery giant John Deere was founded in Illinois in 1837.
- **State Fossil:** The Tully Monster, an odd soft-bodied sea creature from 300 million years ago, is the state fossil.
- **Harpo Studios:** The Oprah Winfrey Show was filmed at Harpo Studios in Chicago from 1986 to 2011.

Indiana

- **Hoosier State:** Indiana is often referred to as the "Hoosier State," although the origin of the term "Hoosier" is unknown.
- **Indy 500:** Indiana is famous for the Indianapolis 500, the world's oldest major automobile race.
- **State Capital:** Indianapolis is the state capital and the largest city in Indiana, and it's one of the largest state capitals in the U.S.
- **Sand Dunes:** The Indiana Dunes, on the shores of Lake Michigan, are the largest collection of sand dunes in the state.
- **Time Zones:** Indiana spans two time zones, Eastern Time and Central Time.
- **Basketball Love:** Basketball is hugely popular in Indiana, which is home to the Indiana Pacers and the NCAA Hall of Champions.
- **James Dean:** Legendary actor James Dean was born in Marion, Indiana in 1931.
- **Farming:** Indiana is a leading producer of corn and soybeans, playing a crucial role in America's agriculture.
- **Notre Dame:** The University of Notre Dame, one of the country's leading Catholic universities, is located in South Bend, Indiana.
- **Covered Bridges:** Parke County, Indiana is considered the "Covered Bridge Capital of the World," with 31 covered bridges.
- **State Bird:** The state bird is the Cardinal, known for its vibrant red color and distinctive crest.
- **Caves:** Indiana is home to numerous caves, including Wyandotte Cave, one of the largest in the U.S.
- **Michael Jackson:** The "King of Pop," Michael Jackson, was born in Gary, Indiana, in 1958.
- **State Tree:** The state tree is the Tulip Tree, known for its distinctive leaf shape and beautiful spring flowers.
- **Zinc Production:** Indiana leads the nation in zinc production, contributing significantly to the state's economy.

- **Purdue University:** Located in West Lafayette, Purdue is a world-renowned university known for its engineering programs.
- **Santa Claus:** There's a town in Indiana named Santa Claus, known for its festive-themed attractions.
- **Amish Population:** Indiana has the second-largest Amish population in the United States.
- **Orville Redenbacher:** Famous popcorn mogul Orville Redenbacher was born in Brazil, Indiana, in 1907.
- **Bloomington:** This city is home to Indiana University, one of the state's leading research institutions.

Iowa

- **Agriculture:** Known as the "Food Capital of the World," Iowa is a leading producer of corn, soybeans, and pork in the U.S.
- **Capitol Building:** Iowa's state capitol in Des Moines is the only one in the U.S. with five domes.
- **Mississippi River:** Iowa's eastern border is formed by the Mississippi River, one of the longest rivers in North America.
- **State Fair:** The Iowa State Fair is one of the largest in the U.S., featuring the famous Butter Cow sculpture.
- **Loess Hills:** These are a formation of wind-deposited loess soil along the westernmost part of Iowa, known for their unique beauty.
- **Presidential Primaries:** Iowa is known for its early presidential primaries, giving it a significant role in U.S. politics.
- **Herbert Hoover:** The 31st President of the U.S., Herbert Hoover, was born in West Branch, Iowa.
- **Population Density:** Iowa has one of the lowest population densities in the country.
- **Field of Dreams:** This iconic baseball field movie set is located in Dyersville, Iowa.
- **Effigy Mounds National Monument:** This monument contains prehistoric mounds built by Native American cultures.
- **John Wayne:** The legendary actor was born in Winterset, Iowa in 1907.
- **Wind Energy:** Iowa is one of the top U.S. states in producing wind energy.
- **RAGBRAI:** The Register's Annual Great Bicycle Ride Across Iowa (RAGBRAI) is the longest, largest, and oldest bicycle touring event in the world.
- **Ames Laboratory:** This U.S. Department of Energy national laboratory located in Ames, Iowa is known for its research in material sciences.

- **Amana Colonies:** These seven villages were built by German Pietists in the 19th century and are now a major tourist attraction.
- **Drake University:** This private university in Des Moines, Iowa is known for its law school and pharmacy program.
- **Slipknot:** The famous heavy metal band was formed in Des Moines, Iowa in 1995.
- **Quaker Oats:** Located in Cedar Rapids, the Quaker Oats facility is the largest cereal company in the world.
- **Hawkeye State:** Iowa is commonly referred to as the "Hawkeye State" as a tribute to chief Black Hawk.
- **Braille:** The Iowa Braille and Sight Saving School in Vinton is where the famous author Laura Ingalls Wilder's sister, Mary, attended after losing her sight.

Kansas

- **Geographical Center:** The geographical center of the 48 contiguous United States is located in Kansas.
- **Sunflower State:** Known as the Sunflower State, Kansas grows more sunflowers than any other U.S. state.
- **Wheat Production:** Kansas is the nation's largest producer of wheat, earning it the nickname "the breadbasket of the world".
- **Dodge City:** Known as the "Cowboy Capital," Dodge City has a rich history in the American Old West.
- **Helium Discovery:** The element helium was first discovered in Kansas in one of the state's natural gas fields.
- **Amelia Earhart:** The pioneering aviator, the first woman to fly solo across the Atlantic, was born in Atchison, Kansas.
- **Salt Mines:** The Kansas Underground Salt Museum in Hutchinson is built within one of the world's largest deposits of rock salt.
- **Brown v. Board of Education:** The landmark Supreme Court case that ended racial segregation in public schools began in Topeka, Kansas.
- **Yellow Brick Road:** Liberal, Kansas hosts a replica of Dorothy's house from The Wizard of Oz and a Yellow Brick Road.
- **First Pizza Hut:** The world's first Pizza Hut opened in Wichita, Kansas, in 1958.
- **Buffalo Bill:** Famed showman and buffalo hunter Buffalo Bill Cody was a resident of Kansas.
- **World's Largest Ball of Twine:** Located in Cawker City, Kansas, it's one of several places claiming this record.
- **Tallgrass Prairie:** Kansas is home to the Tallgrass Prairie National Preserve, the only such preserve in the U.S.
- **Monument Rocks:** These stunning geological formations are one of the Eight Wonders of Kansas.

- **Wind Energy:** Kansas ranks high among U.S. states in wind power generation.
- **Barbed Wire:** The invention of barbed wire, which transformed American agriculture, is celebrated at the Kansas Barbed Wire Museum.
- **Aviation Hub:** Wichita, Kansas is known as the "Air Capital of the World" due to its significant aviation manufacturing history.
- **Prohibition Era:** Carry Nation, a famous figure of the Prohibition Era, started her campaign against alcohol in Medicine Lodge, Kansas.
- **White Castle:** The fast-food hamburger chain White Castle was originally founded in Wichita, Kansas in 1921.
- **Kansas Cosmosphere:** This space museum in Hutchinson houses the largest collection of Russian space artifacts outside of Moscow.

Kentucky

- **Horse Capital:** Lexington, Kentucky, is known as the "Horse Capital of the World."
- **Bluegrass State:** Named after the bluegrass found in many of its pastures due to the fertile soil.
- **Kentucky Derby:** The famous horse race, the Kentucky Derby, is held annually in Louisville, Kentucky.
- **Mammoth Cave:** The world's longest cave system, Mammoth Cave, is located in Kentucky.
- **Bourbon Production:** More than 95% of the world's bourbon is made in Kentucky.
- **Fort Knox:** Home to the U.S. Bullion Depository, which stores a large portion of the country's gold reserves.
- **KFC Origin:** Kentucky is where Colonel Harland Sanders first served his Kentucky Fried Chicken, now a global fast-food franchise.
- **Birthplace of Abraham Lincoln:** The 16th president of the United States, Abraham Lincoln, was born in Hodgenville, Kentucky.
- **The Cumberland Gap:** This natural pass through the Appalachian Mountains was used by Native Americans and early European explorers.
- **Land Between the Lakes:** A national recreation area between Kentucky and Tennessee that is one of the largest blocks of undeveloped forest in the eastern United States.
- **Coal Production:** Kentucky is one of the top three coal-producing states in the U.S.
- **The Corvette Factory:** The only place in the world where the Chevrolet Corvette is produced is in Bowling Green, Kentucky.
- **The Kentucky River:** This tributary of the Ohio River is over 250 miles long and is home to more than 50 species of fish.

- **Daniel Boone:** Famed American pioneer, Daniel Boone, established Boonesborough, Kentucky, one of the first English-speaking settlements beyond the Appalachian Mountains.
- **Kentucky Colonels:** An honorary title bestowed by the Governor of Kentucky, recipients include Muhammad Ali and Winston Churchill.
- **Appalachian Mountains:** Eastern Kentucky is home to the Appalachian Mountains, one of the oldest mountain ranges on Earth.
- **Stephen Foster:** Composer of "My Old Kentucky Home," which is the state song of Kentucky.
- **Red River Gorge:** Known for its abundant natural stone arches and sandstone cliffs, it's a popular destination for rock climbing.
- **Pikeville Cut-Through:** One of the largest civil engineering projects in the western hemisphere, this rock cut was created to reroute the Levisa Fork River.
- **Blue Licks Battlefield:** Site of the last battle of the Revolutionary War in Kentucky.

Louisiana

- **French Influence:** Louisiana was named in honor of King Louis XIV of France.
- **New Orleans:** Known for its unique culture, music, and Mardi Gras festival, New Orleans is one of the most vibrant cities in the U.S.
- **Cajun and Creole Cuisine:** Famous for dishes like gumbo, jambalaya, and crawfish étouffée.
- **Bayou Country:** Known for its marshy, slow-moving waterways known as bayous.
- **Louisiana Purchase:** In 1803, the U.S. acquired Louisiana from France, effectively doubling the size of the nation.
- **Mississippi River:** A major U.S. river, it flows along the eastern border of Louisiana into the Gulf of Mexico.
- **Jazz Birthplace:** New Orleans is widely acknowledged as the birthplace of jazz music.
- **Crawfish Capital:** Louisiana is the largest producer of crawfish in the world.
- **Louisiana State University:** One of the most popular universities in the U.S., it's known for its sports teams, the LSU Tigers.
- **Sugar Production:** Louisiana is one of the top sugar-cane producing states in the U.S.
- **Swamp Tours:** Boat tours of the Louisiana swamps are a popular tourist activity.
- **Tabasco Sauce:** Made on Avery Island, Louisiana, since 1868, Tabasco sauce is known worldwide.
- **Acadian Culture:** The Cajun people, descendants of French Acadians, have a distinct culture and dialect.
- **Spanish Rule:** Louisiana was a Spanish colony from 1762 to 1802.

- **Hurricane Katrina:** In 2005, this devastating hurricane caused significant damage, especially to New Orleans.
- **Louis Armstrong:** Born in New Orleans, he's one of the most influential figures in jazz history.
- **Superdome:** The largest fixed dome structure in the world, it's home to the New Orleans Saints NFL team.
- **Creole Heritage:** The Creole people of Louisiana have a rich heritage, originating from colonial settlers of French, Spanish, African, and Native American descent.
- **Baton Rouge:** The capital of Louisiana, its name means "Red Stick" in French.
- **The French Quarter:** The oldest neighborhood in New Orleans, known for its vibrant nightlife and colorful architecture.

Maine

- **Pine Tree State:** Maine is known as the Pine Tree State, with forests covering 83% of the land area.
- **Lobster Capital:** Maine is a premier source of lobsters in the U.S, providing about 80% of the country's lobsters.
- **Acadia National Park:** Maine's National Park, Acadia, is the first National Park east of the Mississippi River.
- **Stephen King:** This acclaimed horror and suspense author was born and resides in Maine.
- **Largest Coastline:** After Alaska and Florida, Maine has the third-longest coastline in the U.S.
- **Blueberries Production:** Maine produces 98% of the country's lowbush blueberries, also known as "wild" blueberries.
- **The Appalachian Trail:** The eastern terminus of this iconic hiking trail is located at Mount Katahdin in Maine.
- **L.L.Bean:** This famous outdoor retailer was founded in Freeport, Maine in 1912.
- **Moose Population:** Maine has the highest moose population in the lower 48 states.
- **First Sunrise:** The city of Eastport sees the first sunrise in the U.S., due to its easternmost location.
- **Potato Production:** Aroostook County, Maine is one of the largest potato-producing regions in the U.S.
- **Portland:** The city of Portland is known for its vibrant food and craft beer scene.
- **White Mountains:** The state is home to a portion of this mountain range, which stretches across northern New Hampshire.
- **Maple Syrup:** Maine is one of the top maple syrup-producing states in the U.S.

- **Mystery Novels:** Maine serves as the setting for many popular mystery novels, including those by authors like Tess Gerritsen and Paul Doiron.
- **Lighthouses:** Maine is home to 65 historical lighthouses along its rugged coast.
- **Penobscot Narrows Bridge:** This bridge boasts one of the world's longest spans for a cable-stayed bridge.
- **Wildlife:** Maine's diverse habitats are home to species such as black bears, lynx, and a variety of seabirds.
- **Colleges:** Maine has some esteemed higher learning institutions, including Bowdoin College, Bates College, and Colby College.
- **Old Orchard Beach:** A popular summer resort town known for its seven-mile-long beach.

Maryland

- **Founding:** Maryland, established in 1634, is one of the original thirteen colonies.
- **Maryland's Nickname:** Known as the "Old Line State," a reference to its regular line troops who served in the Revolutionary War.
- **US Anthem:** Francis Scott Key penned "The Star-Spangled Banner" in Baltimore during the War of 1812.
- **Oyster Production:** The Chesapeake Bay in Maryland is one of the largest producers of oysters in the world.
- **State Sport:** Maryland's official state sport is jousting, dating back to 1962.
- **Academic Excellence:** The Johns Hopkins University in Baltimore is renowned globally for its programs in medicine and public health.
- **Culinary Delight:** Maryland is famous for its blue crabs, a beloved culinary staple in the state.
- **Underwater City:** The lost city of Aberdeen Proving Ground lies underwater in the Chesapeake Bay.
- **Historic Ships:** Baltimore's Inner Harbor is home to the historic U.S.S. Constellation and U.S.S. Torsk.
- **Historic Site:** Annapolis, the state capital, boasts more 18th century structures than any other U.S. city.
- **Wartime Hospital:** During the Civil War, the U.S. Naval Academy in Annapolis was used as a hospital.
- **Mason-Dixon Line:** The northern border of Maryland is marked by the Mason-Dixon Line.
- **Monocacy Aqueduct:** Maryland houses the largest aqueduct in the U.S, built in the 19th century.
- **American Railroad:** The Baltimore and Ohio (B&O) Railroad, the first long-distance railroad in the U.S., started in Baltimore, Maryland.

- **Religious Freedom:** Maryland was established as a place for religious tolerance and freedom for English Catholics.
- **Wealthy State:** According to U.S. Census data, Maryland has the highest median household income among states.
- **Presidential Retreat:** Camp David, the President's country retreat, is located in Maryland's Catoctin Mountain Park.
- **Port of Baltimore:** The Port of Baltimore is one of America's oldest seaports.
- **Black-Eyed Susan:** The state flower of Maryland is the black-eyed Susan.
- **Thoroughbred Horses:** Maryland's state horse is the Thoroughbred, known for racing and equestrian events.

Massachusetts

- **Mayflower:** In 1620, the Pilgrims landed at Plymouth Rock, initiating the state's rich history.
- **American Revolution:** The Revolutionary War began in Massachusetts with the "Shot Heard Round the World" in Lexington and Concord.
- **Harvard University:** Established in 1636, Harvard is the oldest institution of higher learning in the U.S.
- **Thanksgiving:** The first Thanksgiving Day was celebrated in Plymouth, Massachusetts, in 1621.
- **Basketball Birthplace:** Basketball was invented in 1891 by James Naismith in Springfield, Massachusetts.
- **Boston Tea Party:** In 1773, American patriots staged a protest known as the Boston Tea Party, a major event leading up to the Revolution.
- **Fig Newtons:** Named after the city of Newton, these cookies were invented in Massachusetts.
- **MIT:** The Massachusetts Institute of Technology, founded in 1861, is one of the world's leading scientific and technological research universities.
- **Volleyball Origins:** Volleyball was invented in 1895 in Holyoke, Massachusetts.
- **Salem Witch Trials:** The infamous Salem Witch Trials occurred in Massachusetts in the 17th century.
- **Oldest Public Park:** Boston Common, established in 1634, is America's oldest public park.
- **Whaling Hub:** The city of New Bedford served as the global center of the whaling industry in the 19th century.
- **Birthplace of U.S. Presidents:** Massachusetts is the birthplace of four U.S. Presidents: John Adams, John Quincy Adams, John F. Kennedy, and George H.W. Bush.

- **State Dessert:** The official state dessert of Massachusetts is the Boston Cream Pie.
- **First Public School:** The first public school in America, Boston Latin School, was established in Massachusetts in 1635.
- **Cape Cod:** Cape Cod is a popular summer vacation destination known for its beaches and quaint New England towns.
- **World's Largest Air-Force Base:** Hanscom Air Force Base in Massachusetts is the world's largest air-force base by area.
- **First Subway:** The country's first subway system was built in Boston, Massachusetts in 1897.
- **Paul Revere:** Famous patriot Paul Revere embarked on his historic ride from Boston to Lexington in Massachusetts.
- **Massachusetts Bay Colony:** Established in 1629, the Massachusetts Bay Colony was a major part of the region's early history.

Michigan

- **Great Lakes:** Michigan is the only U.S. state that touches four of the five Great Lakes.
- **Automotive Capital:** Detroit, Michigan is known as the car capital of the world, being home to the "Big Three" car manufacturers.
- **Motown Records:** This iconic record label was founded in Detroit, contributing significantly to the development of American music.
- **Mackinac Bridge:** One of the world's longest suspension bridges, it connects the state's Upper and Lower Peninsulas.
- **Sleeping Bear Dunes:** These impressive sand dunes along Lake Michigan provide a unique landscape and were named "Most Beautiful Place in America" by Good Morning America.
- **Cherry Production:** Michigan is the nation's leading producer of tart cherries, and hosts the National Cherry Festival annually in Traverse City.
- **Kellogg's Cereal:** Battle Creek, Michigan is the birthplace of Kellogg's cereal.
- **Largest City:** Detroit is the largest city in Michigan and the tenth largest in the U.S.
- **Keweenaw Peninsula:** This region is known for its historic copper mining and beautiful scenery.
- **Isle Royale National Park:** This remote island park on Lake Superior is known for its wolf and moose populations.
- **State Stone:** The Petoskey stone, fossilized coral, is Michigan's state stone and can be found along the shores of Lake Michigan.
- **First State to Abolish Death Penalty:** Michigan was the first English-speaking government in the world to abolish capital punishment for ordinary crimes in 1846.
- **Henry Ford Museum:** Located in Dearborn, this museum showcases the evolution of technology and the automobile.

- **Soo Locks:** These locks in Sault Ste. Marie are among the world's busiest, handling ships from the Atlantic to Lake Superior.
- **Faygo Pop:** This popular brand of soda was invented in Detroit.
- **University of Michigan:** This university in Ann Arbor is one of the nation's leading research institutions.
- **Michigan Stadium:** Known as "The Big House", it's the second largest stadium in the world and home to the Michigan Wolverines.
- **More Lighthouses:** Michigan has more lighthouses than any other state, with over 150 dotting its expansive shorelines.
- **Michigan vs. Ohio War:** The Toledo War was a border dispute between Michigan and Ohio in the 19th century.
- **Detroit Institute of Arts:** This museum is renowned for its diverse collection, including Diego Rivera's Detroit Industry Murals.

Minnesota

- **Land of 10,000 Lakes:** Minnesota has 11,842 lakes over 10 acres in size, more shoreline than California, Florida, and Hawaii combined.
- **Mall of America:** The largest shopping mall in the United States is located in Bloomington, Minnesota.
- **Minnesota State Fair:** This is one of the largest and oldest agricultural and industrial expositions in the country.
- **Mississippi River:** The mighty Mississippi River's headwaters are located at Lake Itasca in Minnesota.
- **Juicy Lucy:** This famous cheese-stuffed hamburger was invented in Minneapolis.
- **Twin Cities:** Minnesota's capital, St. Paul, and its largest city, Minneapolis, are known as the Twin Cities.
- **SPAM Museum:** The SPAM Museum, dedicated to the canned meat product, is located in Austin, Minnesota.
- **F. Scott Fitzgerald:** The famous author was born in St. Paul and wrote his first novel there.
- **Mayo Clinic:** The internationally renowned medical center is based in Rochester, Minnesota.
- **Rollerblade:** The company that popularized the rollerblades was founded in Minnesota.
- **Minnehaha Falls:** This notable waterfall is located in Minneapolis and was immortalized in "The Song of Hiawatha."
- **Bob Dylan:** The influential musician was born in Duluth and raised in Hibbing.
- **Wolves:** Minnesota has the largest population of wolves in the lower 48 states.
- **Oldest Rock:** Some of the oldest rock on earth, over 3.5 billion years old, can be found in the Minnesota River valley.
- **The Boundary Waters:** This beautiful canoe area wilderness has over a thousand miles of canoe routes.

- **Paul Bunyan and Babe the Blue Ox:** The famous tall tale characters have a statue in Bemidji.
- **Tonka Trucks:** These popular toys were first manufactured in Mound, Minnesota.
- **Minnesota Orchestra:** This orchestra is one of the top-rated in the nation.
- **Prince:** The music icon was born in Minneapolis and his studio, Paisley Park, is in Chanhassen.
- **Stone Arch Bridge:** This iconic bridge over the Mississippi River in Minneapolis is a symbol of the city.

Mississippi

- **Magnolia State:** Mississippi is known as the Magnolia State due to the abundance of magnolia flowers and trees.
- **River Traffic:** Mississippi River is one of the busiest waterways in terms of cargo carried worldwide.
- **Coca-Cola Origin:** The world's first Coca-Cola Bottling plant outside Atlanta was established in Vicksburg, Mississippi.
- **Biloxi:** This city is considered the birthplace of the Mardi Gras celebration in the United States.
- **Delta Blues:** Mississippi is recognized as the birthplace of the Delta Blues, with notable artists like Muddy Waters and B.B. King hailing from here.
- **Literary Legends:** Mississippi has been home to several Pulitzer Prize-winning authors, including Tennessee Williams and Eudora Welty.
- **Elvis Presley:** The King of Rock 'n Roll was born in Tupelo, Mississippi in 1935.
- **Catfish Capital:** Mississippi farms more than half of the country's farm-raised catfish.
- **Choctaw Indians:** The world's oldest game, Stickball, was originated by the Choctaw Indians of Mississippi.
- **Mississippi Delta:** This region has been called "the most Southern place on earth."
- **Jackson:** The capital city is named after Andrew Jackson, the seventh President of the United States.
- **USS Mississippi:** The battleship served in the Pacific theater during World War II.
- **Natchez Trace Parkway:** This historic 444-mile recreational road links Natchez with Nashville, Tennessee.
- **First Lung Transplant:** The world's first lung transplant was performed at the University of Mississippi Medical Center in 1963.

- **First Heart Transplant:** Mississippi also performed the world's first heart transplant surgery in 1964.
- **Vicksburg National Military Park:** This site commemorates the Battle of Vicksburg during the American Civil War.
- **Frog Capital:** Rayne, a city in Mississippi, is known as the Frog Capital of the World.
- **Teddy Bears:** The Teddy Bear's origin story traces back to a hunting trip Theodore Roosevelt took in Mississippi.
- **International Ballet Competition:** This competition, one of the most prestigious in the world, is held in Jackson every four years.
- **Agriculture:** Mississippi is a leading producer of cotton, soybeans, and rice in the United States.

Missouri

- **Gateway Arch:** Standing at 630 feet, the Gateway Arch in St. Louis is the tallest man-made monument in the U.S.
- **Show-Me State:** Missouri's unofficial nickname is the "Show-Me State," suggesting Missourians are skeptics who need proof before belief.
- **Pony Express:** The Pony Express mail service started in St. Joseph, Missouri, in 1860.
- **Anheuser-Busch:** This beer giant, known for Budweiser, originated in St. Louis and is a major employer in the state.
- **Kansas City BBQ:** Known for its slow-smoked barbecue style, KC has more than 100 barbecue restaurants.
- **Mark Twain:** The celebrated author was born in Florida, Missouri, and drew inspiration from his childhood state.
- **Ozark Mountains:** A large portion of this mountainous region resides in Missouri, providing a rich backdrop of nature and outdoor activities.
- **Lewis and Clark:** The famous expedition set out from St. Louis in 1804, exploring the newly acquired western territory.
- **Jesse James:** The notorious outlaw and gang leader was born and died in Missouri.
- **Forest Park:** Located in St. Louis, it's one of the largest urban parks in the U.S., outstripping New York's Central Park.
- **Harry S Truman:** The 33rd President of the United States was born in Lamar, Missouri.
- **Mississippi River:** Along Missouri's eastern border, it is the second-longest river in North America.
- **Saint Louis Zoo:** One of the nation's top-ranked zoos, it remains free to the public.
- **Ice Cream Cone:** The waffle ice cream cone was first sold at the 1904 World's Fair in St. Louis.

- **Missouri River:** The longest river in North America begins in Montana and enters the Mississippi River north of St. Louis.
- **Branson:** This city is known for its vibrant music scene, with dozens of theaters featuring live music, comedy, and drama.
- **Scott Joplin:** Known as the "King of Ragtime," this composer called Missouri his home.
- **Winston Churchill:** In Fulton, Churchill delivered his famous "Iron Curtain" speech in 1946.
- **Potosi:** This town was originally settled as a lead mining community and was for a time the largest city west of the Mississippi.
- **George Washington Carver:** This renowned scientist started his education at Simpson College in Indianola, Missouri.

Montana

- **Big Sky Country:** Montana's nickname originates from its unobstructed skyline that seems to overwhelm the landscape.
- **Yellowstone:** America's first national park spills over into Montana's southern border.
- **Glacier National Park:** Often referred to as the "Crown of the Continent," the park encompasses over a million acres, 130 named lakes, and hundreds of species of animals.
- **Largest State:** Montana is the fourth largest state in terms of area, but 44th in population density.
- **Bitterroot:** The Bitterroot Valley was originally inhabited by the Salish tribe, and the bitterroot plant is now the state flower.
- **Gold Rush:** Gold was discovered in Grasshopper Creek in 1862, leading to a rush of prospectors into Montana.
- **Dinosaurs:** Montana is a leading state for dinosaur fossils discoveries, including the first identified Tyrannosaurus rex.
- **Battle of Little Bighorn:** The historic 1876 battle, also known as "Custer's Last Stand," took place in southeastern Montana.
- **Continental Divide:** This divide runs north and south through the state, determining the directional flow of rivers.
- **Flathead Lake:** The largest natural freshwater lake in the U.S. west of the Mississippi is found in Montana.
- **Biggest County:** At nearly 5,000 square miles, Beaverhead County, Montana, is larger than the entire state of Connecticut.
- **Jeannette Rankin:** The first woman elected to Congress was from Missoula, Montana.
- **Yogo Sapphires:** Among the finest sapphires in the world, they're found only in Yogo Gulch, Montana.
- **Triple Divide Peak:** One of the few places in North America where water can flow into three different oceans: the Atlantic, the Pacific, and the Arctic.

- **Montana Rockies:** Montana houses over 100 named mountain ranges.
- **Heaven's Peak:** This mountain in Glacier National Park stands at over 8,987 feet tall.
- **Ringling Brothers:** White Sulphur Springs, Montana was the original off-season home for the famous circus.
- **Fort Benton:** Established in 1846, it's the oldest settlement in Montana and was once the "World's Innermost Port."
- **Wheat & Barley:** Montana is a top producer of these crops in the U.S.
- **Blackfeet Nation:** The Blackfeet Reservation is home to the Blackfeet Nation, one of the ten largest tribes in the U.S.

Nebraska

- **Cornhusker State:** Nebraska is known as the Cornhusker State due to its extensive corn farming.
- **Arbor Day:** The tree-planting holiday was started by J. Sterling Morton in Nebraska City in 1872.
- **Chimney Rock:** The most famous landmark for pioneers traveling on the Oregon, California, and Mormon Trails in the 1800s.
- **Sandhill Cranes:** Every spring, the Platte River in central Nebraska sees the world's largest migration of sandhill cranes.
- **Mutual of Omaha:** This Fortune 500 company, known for its insurance and financial services, is based in Nebraska.
- **Henry Doorly Zoo:** Located in Omaha, it's considered one of the world's best zoos with the largest indoor desert and nocturnal exhibits.
- **Kool-Aid:** The popular powdered drink mix was invented in Hastings, Nebraska, in 1927.
- **Nebraska State Capitol:** Notable for its tower structure, it's the second tallest state capitol building in the U.S.
- **Largest Mammoth Fossils:** The University of Nebraska State Museum houses the largest mammoth fossil on record.
- **Carhenge:** A replica of England's Stonehenge constructed with vintage cars, located in Alliance, Nebraska.
- **Buffalo Bill Ranch:** The historic home of showman William F. "Buffalo Bill" Cody is in North Platte.
- **Strategic Air Command:** Offutt Air Force Base near Omaha was the longtime headquarters for this key component of the U.S. military during the Cold War.
- **Center Pivot Irrigation:** Developed in Nebraska in the 1940s, it revolutionized agriculture worldwide.
- **College World Series:** This annual baseball championship has been held in Omaha since 1950.

- **Warren Buffett:** The billionaire investor and philanthropist lives in Omaha, his hometown.
- **Ponca Tribe:** One of the Native American tribes originally from Nebraska; the city of Ponca is named after them.
- **St. Cecilia Cathedral:** One of the largest cathedrals in the U.S., this Spanish Colonial-style structure is in Omaha.
- **Boys Town:** The famous home for troubled youth, immortalized in a 1938 movie, is located just west of Omaha.
- **Scotts Bluff:** A National Monument and key landmark on the Oregon Trail, located in western Nebraska.
- **Ak-Sar-Ben:** This Omaha civic organization (its name is "Nebraska" spelled backwards) was influential for over a century.

Nevada

- **Silver State:** Nevada is often referred to as the Silver State due to its significant silver deposits.
- **Area 51:** This secretive U.S. Air Force facility, a focal point of many conspiracy theories, is located in Nevada.
- **Las Vegas Strip:** Famous globally for its concentration of resort hotels and casinos.
- **Reno Air Races:** The world's fastest motorsport, with planes flying wingtip-to-wingtip.
- **Great Basin National Park:** Known for Lehman Caves and ancient bristlecone pines, the oldest trees in the world.
- **Battle Born State:** Nevada's state motto, reflecting its admission to the Union during the Civil War.
- **Hoover Dam:** An engineering marvel, it was the highest concrete dam in the world when completed in 1936.
- **Lake Tahoe:** The largest alpine lake in North America, famous for its clear, deep-blue water.
- **Quick Divorces:** In the early 20th century, Nevada's lenient divorce laws made it a popular place for quick divorces.
- **Atomic Testing Museum:** This Las Vegas museum chronicles the history of nuclear testing at the nearby Nevada Test Site.
- **Burning Man Festival:** This annual event in the Black Rock Desert attracts tens of thousands of participants from around the world.
- **Virginia City:** Once a thriving mining town, it's now a popular tourist destination with well-preserved 19th-century buildings.
- **Pyramid Lake:** This desert lake, a remnant of the ancient Lake Lahontan, is known for its distinctive tufa formations.
- **Sheldon National Wildlife Refuge:** A 575,000-acre refuge home to pronghorn antelope, bighorn sheep, and wild horses.

- **Bellagio Fountains:** A large dancing water fountain synchronized with music, one of the most iconic sights in Las Vegas.
- **Gold Production:** Nevada is the largest gold-producing state in the U.S., and the fourth largest in the world.
- **Largest City by Area:** Las Vegas is the U.S. city with the most land area, spreading over 600 square miles.
- **The Neon Boneyard:** This outdoor museum in Las Vegas is home to many of the city's iconic retired neon signs.
- **Red Rock Canyon:** A stunning natural area known for its towering red sandstone peaks and Native American petroglyphs.
- **Bodie Flats:** Named after a Paiute tribe leader, this area is the site of a proposed Indian reservation in the 1870s.

New Hampshire

- **Granite State:** New Hampshire is nicknamed the "Granite State" for its extensive granite formations and quarries.
- **First in the Nation:** New Hampshire holds the first primary in the U.S. presidential election cycle.
- **Mount Washington:** The highest peak in the northeastern U.S., it's known for its dangerously erratic weather.
- **First American in Space:** Alan Shepard, the first American in space, was born in Derry, New Hampshire.
- **Algonquin Language:** "New Hampshire" comes from the language of the area's Algonquin-speaking native peoples.
- **Maple Syrup:** New Hampshire is famous for its high-quality maple syrup, with sugaring events every spring.
- **Nashua River:** This formerly polluted waterway is now a highlight of environmental restoration efforts.
- **Franconia Notch:** A spectacular mountain pass in the White Mountains, home to the former Old Man of the Mountain.
- **White Mountains:** A popular recreational area, it's part of the northern Appalachian Mountains.
- **Skiing Tradition:** New Hampshire has a rich history of skiing with over 30 alpine and cross-country ski resorts.
- **Covered Bridges:** The state has 54 historic covered bridges, a charming element of its rural landscapes.
- **Dartmouth College:** An Ivy League university, it's the ninth-oldest institution of higher learning in the U.S.
- **Motorcycle Week:** Laconia Motorcycle Week is one of the largest and oldest motorcycle rallies in the world.
- **Canterbury Shaker Village:** One of the best-preserved Shaker sites, offering insights into this religious community's life.
- **Paper Birch:** The state tree of New Hampshire, known for its distinctive white bark.

- **Lake Winnipesaukee:** The largest lake in New Hampshire, a beloved destination for boating, fishing, and watersports.
- **Pumpkin Festival:** This annual event in Laconia holds the world record for most lit jack-o'-lanterns on display.
- **Portsmouth Harbor:** Known for its historic seaport, featuring beautifully preserved 18th-century buildings.
- **Purple Lilac:** New Hampshire's state flower, chosen for its hardiness and the ideals of independence it represents.
- **Colonial History:** Portsmouth's Strawbery Banke is an outdoor museum of 32 historic buildings from the colonial era.

New Jersey

- **Garden State:** New Jersey is known as the "Garden State" due to its rich agricultural heritage.
- **First Diner:** The first ever "diner" was created in Newark, New Jersey, in 1871.
- **Diverse Population:** It's the most densely populated state in the U.S., and one of the most culturally diverse.
- **Thomas Edison's Lab:** The famous inventor's laboratory was located in Menlo Park, New Jersey.
- **Jersey Shore:** The state boasts 130 miles of beautiful coastline, popular for beaches and boardwalks.
- **Blueberry Capital:** Hammonton, in Atlantic County, is considered the blueberry capital of the world.
- **Liberty State Park:** Located in Jersey City, it offers stunning views of the Statue of Liberty and Manhattan skyline.
- **Princeton University:** One of the Ivy League universities, it's consistently ranked among the top universities worldwide.
- **Lucy the Elephant:** A unique piece of roadside Americana, located in Margate and standing six stories high.
- **Pine Barrens:** A large and mysterious expanse of sandy soil and pine forests, full of legends and folklore.
- **Record Breaking Boardwalk:** The longest boardwalk in the world is located in Atlantic City.
- **First Drive-In Movie:** The world's first drive-in movie theater opened in Camden, New Jersey, in 1933.
- **Paterson Great Falls:** One of the largest waterfalls in the U.S. and a national historic park.
- **Miss America Pageant:** First held in Atlantic City in 1921, it's one of the nation's longest-running beauty pageants.
- **First Baseball Game:** The first organized baseball game was played in Hoboken in 1846.

- **Cape May:** Known for its Victorian architecture, it's the oldest seaside resort in the U.S.
- **Submarine Birthplace:** The first successful submarine ride was taken in the Passaic River.
- **Horse Racing History:** Monmouth Park Racetrack in Oceanport opened in 1870 and continues to host prestigious races.
- **Largest Port:** The Port of New York and New Jersey is the largest port on the East Coast.
- **Grover Cleveland Birthplace:** The 22nd and 24th U.S. President was born in Caldwell.

New Mexico

- **State Nickname:** Known as the "Land of Enchantment" for its scenic beauty and rich history.
- **Roswell Incident:** The town of Roswell is world-renowned for a reported UFO crash in 1947.
- **Carlsbad Caverns:** One of the most impressive cave systems in the world, with over 119 known caves.
- **White Sands:** Home to the world's largest gypsum dune field, covering 275 square miles.
- **Manhattan Project:** Los Alamos was the birthplace of the atomic bomb during World War II.
- **Hot Air Ballooning:** Albuquerque hosts the world's largest hot air balloon festival each year.
- **Native American Pueblos:** New Mexico is home to 19 pueblos that have preserved their unique culture and traditions.
- **Chile Capital:** Known as the "Chile Capital of the World," Hatch is famous for its flavorful green chiles.
- **Oldest House:** The oldest house in the U.S., built in 1646, is located in Santa Fe.
- **Taos Pueblo:** One of the oldest continuously inhabited communities in the United States.
- **Chaco Canyon:** An important ancestral Puebloan cultural site, now a UNESCO World Heritage Site.
- **Bandelier National Monument:** Home to ancestral Pueblo dwellings built into the soft cliff rock.
- **Very Large Array:** An astronomical radio observatory consisting of 27 large antennas near Socorro.
- **Georgia O'Keeffe Museum:** Santa Fe museum dedicated to the work of the American modernist artist.
- **Petroglyph National Monument:** Over 20,000 ancient symbols or 'petroglyphs' were carved into volcanic rock by Native Americans and Spanish settlers.

- **Smoky Bear:** The living symbol of forest fire prevention was a black bear cub found in the Capitan Mountains.
- **Billy the Kid:** This infamous outlaw's grave is located in Fort Sumner.
- **Oldest Capital City:** Santa Fe is the oldest state capital in the U.S., founded in 1610.
- **The Pecos River:** This river runs through the state, offering opportunities for fishing and boating.
- **Sandia Peak Tramway:** The world's third-longest single span tramway, offering stunning views of Albuquerque.

New York

- **Empire State Building:** This iconic skyscraper was the world's tallest building from 1931 to 1970.
- **Statue of Liberty:** A gift from France, it's a symbol of freedom and democracy worldwide.
- **Central Park:** The most visited urban park in the U.S. covers 843 acres in Manhattan.
- **Niagara Falls:** One of the world's most famous waterfalls, located on the border with Canada.
- **Broadway:** The highest level of commercial theater in the world, with 41 professional theaters.
- **Times Square:** Known as "The Crossroads of the World," it's one of the busiest pedestrian intersections globally.
- **Wall Street:** The heart of the U.S. financial district, housing the New York Stock Exchange.
- **Adirondack Park:** The largest publicly protected area in the continental U.S., larger than Yellowstone, Everglades, Glacier, and Grand Canyon parks combined.
- **Coney Island:** A popular seaside resort, it's recognized for its amusement parks and iconic hot dogs.
- **Finger Lakes:** A group of 11 long, narrow lakes in central New York, known for their wineries.
- **Erie Canal:** Opened in 1825, it played a critical role in westward expansion and the state's economic growth.
- **New York Public Library:** One of the largest public libraries in the world, with over 53 million items.
- **United Nations Headquarters:** New York City is home to the global headquarters of the UN.
- **Ellis Island:** From 1892 to 1954, it was the busiest immigrant inspection station in the U.S.
- **Metropolitan Museum of Art:** One of the world's largest and finest art museums.

- **One World Trade Center:** The main building of the rebuilt World Trade Center complex, and the tallest building in the Western Hemisphere.
- **Brooklyn Bridge:** Completed in 1883, it was the first steel-wire suspension bridge constructed.
- **Baseball Hall of Fame:** Located in Cooperstown, it honors the history of baseball and its greatest players.
- **New York Fashion Week:** One of the world's four major fashion weeks, it's held twice a year.
- **Grand Central Terminal:** A famous landmark and transportation hub, known for its architecture and ceiling depicting celestial bodies.

North Carolina

- **First in Flight:** The Wright Brothers conducted their first successful powered flight in Kitty Hawk, NC in 1903.
- **Biltmore Estate:** The largest privately-owned house in the U.S., built by George Washington Vanderbilt II.
- **Cape Hatteras Lighthouse:** The tallest brick lighthouse in the U.S., protecting one of the most hazardous sections of the Atlantic Coast.
- **Research Triangle Park:** One of the largest research parks in the world, home to over 200 companies.
- **Blue Ridge Parkway:** Known as "America's Favorite Drive," offers stunning views of the Appalachian Highlands.
- **Great Smoky Mountains National Park:** The most visited national park in the U.S., famous for its diversity of plant and animal life.
- **NASCAR Birthplace:** The first NASCAR race was held on June 19, 1949, at Charlotte Speedway.
- **University of North Carolina:** Chartered in 1789, it's one of the oldest public universities in the U.S.
- **Cherokee Indian Reservation:** The Eastern Band of Cherokee Indians' home, preserving native culture and history.
- **Asheville's Craft Beer Scene:** The city has the most breweries per capita of any U.S. city.
- **Pepsi Creation:** The popular soft drink was first invented and served in New Bern in 1898.
- **Blackbeard's Ship:** The notorious pirate's flagship, the Queen Anne's Revenge, was found off the coast in 1996.
- **Venus Flytrap Origin:** This carnivorous plant is native to the wetlands in the coastal regions of NC.
- **Bodie Island Lighthouse:** One of the famous Outer Banks lighthouses, known for its distinct horizontal stripes.

- **Appalachian Trail:** A portion of this scenic long-distance hiking trail runs through NC.
- **Lexington Barbecue:** Known as the "Barbecue Capital of the World," Lexington hosts an annual Barbecue Festival.
- **Pinehurst Resort:** Known as the "Cradle of American Golf," it has hosted more golf championships than any other site in the U.S.
- **Cape Lookout National Seashore:** Home to wild horses and the Cape Lookout Lighthouse.
- **Grandfather Mountain:** Known for its mile-high swinging bridge, wildlife habitats, and hiking trails.
- **Hungry Mother State Park:** The park got its unique name from a local legend.

North Dakota

- **Flickertail State:** North Dakota is nicknamed after the Richardson ground squirrels commonly found within the state.
- **Roughrider Country:** Another nickname for the state is in honor of the volunteer cavalry regiment led by Teddy Roosevelt during the Spanish-American War.
- **Center of North America:** The geographic center of North America is located near the town of Rugby, ND.
- **Dakota Gasification Company:** The only synthetic natural gas producer in the U.S., turning coal into gas.
- **Badlands:** The North Dakota Badlands are home to the state's highest point, White Butte.
- **Garrison Dam:** The fifth-largest earthen dam in the U.S., creating Lake Sakakawea.
- **Agricultural Powerhouse:** North Dakota leads the nation in the production of several crops, including spring wheat, sunflowers, and flaxseed.
- **Chokecherry State:** North Dakota's state fruit is the chokecherry, used in wines, jams, jellies, and syrups.
- **Fargo Theatre:** A restored 1926 Art Deco movie palace that hosts a variety of cultural events.
- **Salem Sue:** The world's largest Holstein cow statue, located in New Salem.
- **North Dakota Heritage Center:** The state's largest museum, highlighting over 600 million years of history.
- **Fort Abraham Lincoln:** The site where Lt. Col. George Armstrong Custer and the 7th Cavalry embarked on their ill-fated journey to Little Big Horn.
- **Enchanted Highway:** A collection of giant scrap metal sculptures along an otherwise desolate stretch of road.
- **Milk Production:** North Dakota is a leading state for milk production, particularly from its large dairy farms.

- **Oil Boom:** The Bakken oil boom resulted in a rapid rise in the state's population and economy in the early 21st century.
- **North Dakota State University:** Home to the NDSU Bison, the football team with the most championships in FCS history.
- **Maah Daah Hey Trail:** One of the longest single-track mountain biking trails in the U.S.
- **Peace Garden State:** The International Peace Garden straddles the border between North Dakota and Manitoba, Canada, symbolizing peace between the nations.
- **Teddy Roosevelt's Ranch:** Roosevelt ranched in the Badlands, and the land is now a national park named in his honor.
- **Scandinavian Heritage:** The state hosts a large Scandinavian-American population and hosts an annual Norsk Hostfest.

Ohio

- **Birthplace of Presidents:** Ohio is often called the "Mother of Presidents" as it is the birthplace of seven U.S. Presidents.
- **Rock and Roll Capital:** Cleveland, Ohio is home to the Rock and Roll Hall of Fame.
- **Roller Coaster Haven:** Cedar Point in Sandusky, Ohio is renowned for its record-breaking roller coasters.
- **Cuyahoga River Fire:** The river once famously caught fire due to pollution, sparking major environmental reforms.
- **Buckeye State:** Named for its abundance of buckeye trees, the seeds of which resemble a deer's eye.
- **Wright Brothers:** The aviation pioneers were from Dayton, Ohio.
- **Zanesville Y-Bridge:** This unique bridge has three ends, looking like the letter "Y" from the air.
- **Hocking Hills State Park:** Known for its spectacular rock formations and waterfalls.
- **Serpent Mound:** The largest effigy mound in the U.S., shaped like a snake swallowing an egg.
- **Pro Football Hall of Fame:** Located in Canton, Ohio, it commemorates the best of professional American football.
- **Lake Erie Shoreline:** Ohio is home to a part of the Great Lakes, offering beautiful beaches and water sports.
- **Kings Island:** A large amusement park, home to one of the world's longest wooden roller coasters.
- **Amish Country:** Holmes County, Ohio has one of the largest Amish populations in the U.S.
- **Tomato Juice:** Ohio designated tomato juice as the official state beverage in 1965.
- **Cincinnati Zoo:** The second-oldest zoo in the U.S, it has been a pioneer in breeding endangered species.
- **First Traffic Light:** The world's first electric traffic signal was put up in Cleveland, Ohio in 1914.

- **The Toledo War:** This was a boundary dispute between Ohio and the Michigan Territory in the 1800s.
- **Ohio and Erie Canal:** The canal was a crucial transport route in the 19th century before the advent of railroads.
- **Neil Armstrong Museum:** The first person to walk on the moon hailed from Wapakoneta, Ohio.
- **Marietta:** This city was the first permanent settlement of the Northwest Territory.

Oklahoma

- **Land Run:** The state was originally settled during the Land Run of 1889, where territories were claimed in a race.
- **Dust Bowl:** Much of Oklahoma was severely affected by the Dust Bowl during the Great Depression.
- **Tornado Alley:** Oklahoma is part of Tornado Alley and experiences an average of 52 tornadoes annually.
- **Oil Production:** Oklahoma is one of the top oil-producing states in the U.S.
- **Native American Population:** Oklahoma has the second-highest Native American population in the U.S.
- **Route 66:** This iconic American highway crosses the state from east to west, linking numerous communities.
- **Oklahoma City Bombing:** The Alfred P. Murrah Federal Building bombing in 1995 remains one of the deadliest terrorist attacks on U.S. soil.
- **Cimarron River:** At 698 miles long, the Cimarron River is one of the longest in the state.
- **National Cowboy & Western Heritage Museum:** Located in Oklahoma City, it's dedicated to preserving the history of the American West.
- **Chickasaw National Recreation Area:** Known for its mineral springs and abundant wildlife.
- **Bison Herds:** Oklahoma has one of the largest bison populations in the country.
- **Red Dirt Music:** A music genre named after the color of soil found in Oklahoma.
- **Oklahoma Panhandle:** This thin strip of land was once called "No Man's Land" as it wasn't part of any state.
- **Tulsa Race Massacre:** One of the worst incidents of racial violence in American history occurred in Tulsa in 1921.

- **State Meal:** Oklahoma's official state meal includes cornbread, barbecued pork, fried okra, and more.
- **Noodling:** This unusual fishing method—catching catfish with bare hands—is a tradition in Oklahoma.
- **OKC Thunder:** Oklahoma City is home to the Thunder, one of the NBA's youngest franchises.
- **Will Rogers:** This famous cowboy, humorist, and actor was from Oklahoma.
- **The Flaming Lips:** This Grammy-winning rock band hails from Oklahoma City.
- **Black Mesa:** At 4,973 feet, Black Mesa is the highest point in Oklahoma.

Oregon

- **Crater Lake:** The deepest lake in the U.S. formed by a volcanic eruption about 7,700 years ago.
- **Portland:** Known as "City of Roses" due to its ideal climate for growing roses.
- **Multnomah Falls:** A two-tier waterfall, reaching a combined height of 620 feet, one of the tallest in the U.S.
- **Beverage Law:** It is illegal in Oregon for a bartender to pour a drink while the glass is in the customer's hand.
- **Public Beaches:** Oregon was the first U.S. state to publicly own its entire coastline.
- **Columbia River:** The 4th largest river in the U.S. by volume, which defines Oregon's northern boundary.
- **Voodoo Doughnut:** An iconic doughnut shop in Portland, known for its unconventional doughnuts.
- **Mt. Hood:** The tallest mountain in Oregon and the second most climbed mountain in the world.
- **Eugene:** Known as "TrackTown USA" and is the birthplace of Nike.
- **Silicon Forest:** The nickname for the cluster of high-tech companies located in the Portland metropolitan area.
- **Naked Bike Ride:** Portland hosts the World Naked Bike Ride annually to promote positive body image.
- **Pinot Noir:** Oregon's Willamette Valley is one of the premier Pinot Noir producing areas in the world.
- **Tillamook Cheese:** This beloved cheese brand originates from Tillamook, Oregon.
- **Powell's Books:** Located in Portland, it's one of the world's largest independent bookstores.
- **Oregon Trail:** A 2,170-mile historic East–West wagon route that connected Missouri to Oregon's Willamette Valley.

- **Animal Law:** In 2014, Oregon became the first state to legalize the therapeutic use of psychedelic mushrooms.
- **Shoe Tree:** There's a tree in Eastern Oregon filled with hundreds of pairs of shoes.
- **Haystack Rock:** This 235-foot sea stack off Cannon Beach is a protected marine and bird sanctuary.
- **Timberline Lodge:** A ski lodge on the south side of Mount Hood and a National Historic Landmark.
- **Marionberry:** A blackberry hybrid developed in Marion County, Oregon, which is a local favorite.

Pennsylvania

- **Liberty Bell:** Iconic symbol of American independence, located in Philadelphia.
- **Independence Hall:** The birthplace of both the Declaration of Independence and the Constitution.
- **Hershey:** Known as "The Sweetest Place on Earth", it's home to Hershey's chocolates.
- **First Zoo:** The Philadelphia Zoo, opened in 1874, is America's first zoo.
- **Punxsutawney Phil:** The famous groundhog that predicts the length of winter every Groundhog Day.
- **Pennsylvania Dutch:** Refers to the German-speaking settlers of Pennsylvania, not the Dutch.
- **Amish Country:** Lancaster County is home to the largest Amish community in the U.S.
- **Cheesesteak:** This iconic sandwich was created in Philadelphia.
- **Rocky Steps:** The steps leading to the Philadelphia Museum of Art, made famous by the "Rocky" movies.
- **Pittsburgh Bridges:** Pittsburgh has 446 bridges, more than any other city in the world.
- **Heinz Ketchup:** Pittsburgh is home to the Heinz company, one of the largest food processing companies in the world.
- **Steel City:** Pittsburgh is historically known for its steel production.
- **Liberty Tunnel:** One of the longest automobile tunnels in the U.S., located in Pittsburgh.
- **Little League:** The world's largest organized youth sports program was started in Williamsport in 1939.
- **First Daily Newspaper:** The Philadelphia Packet and Daily Advertiser, the first daily newspaper in the U.S., was founded in 1784.

- **Benjamin Franklin Parkway:** A scenic boulevard in Philadelphia, modeled after the Champs-Élysées in Paris.
- **Three Rivers:** Pittsburgh is located at the confluence of the Allegheny, Monongahela, and Ohio rivers.
- **Horseshoe Curve:** A world-famous railroad landmark near Altoona.
- **Pennsylvania Turnpike:** Known as "America's First Superhighway."
- **Sylvania:** Pennsylvania's name means "Penn's Woods" or "Penn's Land."

Rhode Island

- **Smallest State:** Rhode Island is the smallest state in the U.S. by land area.
- **Full Name:** It's official name is "The State of Rhode Island and Providence Plantations."
- **Newport Mansions:** These opulent homes were the summer retreats for America's wealthiest families during the Gilded Age.
- **White Horse Tavern:** Located in Newport, it's the oldest tavern building in continuous use in the U.S.
- **America's Cup:** Newport is known for its rich sailing history, notably the prestigious America's Cup yacht race.
- **Narragansett Bay:** This body of water has a surface area of 147 square miles.
- **Independent Man:** The statue atop the State House, symbolizing freedom and independence.
- **Oldest Carousel:** The Flying Horse Carousel in Watch Hill is one of the oldest carousels in the U.S.
- **Coffee Milk:** This unique beverage, made with coffee syrup and milk, is the official state drink.
- **Block Island:** This popular summer tourist destination is known for its beaches, cliffs, and lighthouse.
- **Brown University:** An Ivy League institution and one of the oldest universities in the U.S.
- **Touro Synagogue:** The oldest synagogue in the U.S., located in Newport.
- **WaterFire:** A unique public art installation in Providence with fires on the three rivers downtown.
- **Fort Adams:** A former U.S. Army post in Newport that's the largest coastal fortification in the country.
- **Providence Athenaeum:** One of the oldest libraries in the U.S., founded in 1836.

- **Gilbert Stuart:** This Rhode Island native was a prominent portrait painter, best known for his George Washington portrait.
- **Cumberlandite:** The official state rock, which is only found in large quantities in Rhode Island.
- **Newport Cliff Walk:** A 3.5-mile walking trail that combines stunning ocean views with the architectural history of Newport's gilded age.
- **Roger Williams Park:** A 427-acre park in Providence, featuring a zoo, botanical center, and Museum of Natural History.
- **Rhode Island Red:** The official state bird, a breed of chicken renowned for its egg laying ability.

South Carolina

- **Charleston:** Founded in 1670, it's the oldest city in South Carolina.
- **Fort Sumter:** The Civil War began here in 1861 when Confederate forces fired on the Union garrison.
- **Palmetto Tree:** The official state tree and symbol, known for its importance during the Revolutionary War.
- **Grand Strand:** A 60-mile stretch of beaches along the Atlantic coast that attracts millions of tourists each year.
- **Myrtle Beach:** A popular vacation destination known for its golf courses, amusement parks, and beachfront boardwalk.
- **Gullah Culture:** The Gullah are African Americans who have preserved much of their African linguistic and cultural heritage.
- **Rice Cultivation:** Once the leading rice producer in the U.S., with plantations dominating the coastal areas.
- **Blue Ridge Mountains:** Part of the Appalachian Mountains, they offer spectacular hiking and beautiful scenic views.
- **Clemson University:** A top-25 public university located in the town of Clemson.
- **Hilton Head Island:** Known for its pristine beaches, golf courses, and a distinctive lighthouse.
- **Francis Marion:** Known as the "Swamp Fox," he was a Revolutionary War hero known for his guerrilla warfare.
- **Charleston Tea Plantation:** The only place where tea is grown commercially in the U.S.
- **Spartanburg Peach Festival:** South Carolina produces more peaches than Georgia, the Peach State!
- **Carolina Wren:** This small but boisterous bird is the state bird of South Carolina.
- **Shag Dancing:** A swing dance that's popular along the coast and is the official state dance.

- **Magnolia Plantation:** Founded in 1676, it's one of the oldest public gardens in America.
- **Congaree National Park:** Home to the largest intact expanse of old growth bottomland hardwood forest in the southeastern U.S.
- **Sweetgrass Baskets:** These coiled baskets are a centuries-old tradition among the Gullah people.
- **Arthur Ravenel Jr. Bridge:** A cable-stayed bridge over the Cooper River in Charleston.
- **Beaufort:** The second-oldest city in South Carolina, known for its well-preserved antebellum architecture.

South Dakota

- **Mount Rushmore:** The world-famous monument carved with the faces of four U.S. Presidents.
- **Badlands National Park:** A geologic wonderland of buttes, pinnacles, spires, and mixed-grass prairies.
- **Sioux Falls:** South Dakota's largest city, named after the falls of the Big Sioux River.
- **Sturgis Motorcycle Rally:** An annual gathering attracting hundreds of thousands of motorcycle enthusiasts.
- **Crazy Horse Memorial:** A mountain monument under construction, honoring Oglala Lakota warrior, Crazy Horse.
- **Corn Palace:** A multi-purpose arena in Mitchell decorated with crop art, the only one of its kind.
- **Black Hills:** A small mountain range and home to the sacred ground of the Sioux.
- **Deadwood:** A wild west town and National Historic Landmark known for its gold rush history.
- **Jewel Cave:** The third-longest cave in the world, filled with calcite crystals.
- **Pierre:** The state capital and second smallest by population in the United States.
- **Wind Cave National Park:** One of the oldest national parks in the U.S. and home to the world's densest cave system.
- **Gold Discovery:** Gold was found in the Black Hills in 1874, sparking the Black Hills Gold Rush.
- **Buffalo Roundup:** An annual event in Custer State Park where cowboys and cowgirls roundup and drive the herd of approximately 1,300 buffalo.
- **Rosebud Reservation:** The home of the Sicangu (Brulé) Lakota tribe and the birthplace of activist Leonard Peltier.
- **Wall Drug Store:** A unique shopping mall and tourist attraction located in the town of Wall.

- **Bear Butte State Park:** A sacred site for many indigenous tribes, including the Cheyenne and Lakota.
- **Laura Ingalls Wilder:** The author lived in De Smet, and her famous "Little House on the Prairie" series is based on her childhood experiences.
- **Homestake Mine:** The largest and deepest gold mine in North America until it closed in 2002.
- **Mammoth Site:** A paleontological site and museum in Hot Springs, where Columbian and woolly mammoths have been found.
- **Falls Park:** A park in Sioux Falls surrounding the city's namesake waterfalls.

Tennessee

- **Graceland:** Elvis Presley's iconic home, now a museum, is located in Memphis.
- **Great Smoky Mountains:** America's most visited national park straddles the border between Tennessee and North Carolina.
- **Nashville:** Known as the "Music City", Nashville is considered the heart of the country music industry.
- **Jack Daniel's Distillery:** Located in Lynchburg, it's the oldest registered distillery in the United States.
- **Grand Ole Opry:** The world's longest-running live radio show, showcasing the best in country music.
- **Dollywood:** A theme park in Pigeon Forge co-owned by country music legend Dolly Parton.
- **Tennessee River:** The river flows through Tennessee, Alabama, and Kentucky, covering 652 miles.
- **Parthenon Replica:** Nashville's Centennial Park features a full-scale replica of the Parthenon in Athens.
- **University of Tennessee:** A public research university in Knoxville, home to the Volunteers.
- **Chattanooga Choo Choo:** The historic hotel was once the terminal station for the Southern Railway.
- **Sun Studio:** Known as the "Birthplace of Rock 'n Roll", where Elvis Presley, Johnny Cash, and Jerry Lee Lewis started their careers.
- **Bristol:** Known as the "Birthplace of Country Music", it's where the first commercial recordings of country music were made.
- **Tennessee Valley Authority:** The New Deal-era agency still provides flood control and electricity to the Tennessee Valley.
- **Andrew Jackson's Hermitage:** The former president's plantation is a national landmark outside Nashville.
- **Ruby Falls:** An underground waterfall within Lookout Mountain, near Chattanooga.

- **Belle Meade Plantation:** A historic mansion in Nashville, now a museum dedicated to Southern history.
- **Knoxville World's Fair:** The 1982 World's Fair was held in Knoxville, attracting 11 million visitors.
- **Davy Crockett:** The legendary frontiersman and politician was born in Greene County, Tennessee.
- **Nashville Predators:** The professional ice hockey team based in Nashville.
- **Tennessee Walking Horse:** The state horse, known for its unique four-beat "running walk".

Texas

- **Lone Star State:** Texas' nickname, symbolizing its former status as an independent republic.
- **Alamo Mission:** The site of the famous 1836 Battle of the Alamo in San Antonio.
- **Texas State Capitol:** The largest state capitol building in the United States, located in Austin.
- **Space Center Houston:** The visitor center at NASA's astronaut training and flight control complex.
- **King Ranch:** Larger than the state of Rhode Island, it's one of the largest ranches in the world.
- **Bluebonnet:** The state flower of Texas, known for its vibrant spring blooms.
- **San Jacinto Monument:** The world's tallest masonry column, commemorating the Battle of San Jacinto.
- **Big Bend National Park:** A diverse park with desert, mountain, and river environments.
- **Oil Boom:** Texas experienced a major economic boom when oil was discovered in 1901.
- **Guadalupe Peak:** The highest point in Texas, standing at 8,751 feet above sea level.
- **Dr Pepper:** Invented in Waco in 1885, a year before Coca-Cola was introduced.
- **Texas State Fair:** Held annually at Fair Park in Dallas, it's the largest state fair in the US by annual attendance.
- **Live Music Capital:** Austin is recognized as the Live Music Capital of the World.
- **Dallas Cowboys:** The football team has been valued as the most valuable sports team in the world.
- **Rio Grande:** The river forms part of the Mexico–Texas border.
- **Gonzales Flag:** The "Come and Take It" flag originates from the first battle of the Texas Revolution.

- **Palo Duro Canyon:** Known as the "Grand Canyon of Texas", it's the second largest canyon in the US.
- **Texas Longhorn:** The official state mammal, known for its characteristic horn span.
- **Galveston Hurricane of 1900:** The deadliest natural disaster in US history occurred in Galveston.
- **Bats of Congress Avenue Bridge:** Home to the world's largest urban bat colony in Austin.

Utah

- **Beehive State:** Utah's nickname, symbolizing industry, thrift, and perseverance.
- **Salt Lake City:** The city was founded in 1847 by Brigham Young and other Mormon pioneers.
- **Great Salt Lake:** The largest saltwater lake in the Western Hemisphere.
- **Mormon Influence:** The state is home to The Church of Jesus Christ of Latter-day Saints (LDS Church).
- **Bryce Canyon National Park:** Known for crimson-colored hoodoos, which are spire-shaped rock formations.
- **Promontory Summit:** The location where the First Transcontinental Railroad was completed in 1869.
- **Delicate Arch:** The famous sandstone arch featured on Utah's license plates.
- **Bonneville Salt Flats:** One of the most unique natural features in Utah, where land speed records are often set.
- **Park City:** A city known for its ski resorts and the annual Sundance Film Festival.
- **Rainbow Bridge:** The world's largest known natural bridge, located in southern Utah.
- **Arches National Park:** Home to over 2,000 natural sandstone arches.
- **Mormon Pioneer National Historic Trail:** The route that Brigham Young and the first "Mormon pioneers" took to Utah.
- **Utah's State Bird:** The California gull, credited with saving the Mormon pioneers' crops from a cricket plague in 1848.
- **Zion National Park:** A nature preserve distinguished by steep red cliffs.
- **Kings Peak:** The highest point in Utah, standing at 13,534 feet.
- **Utah Jazz:** The state's NBA basketball team, originally from New Orleans.

- **Navajo Sandstone:** A geological formation found in the southern and east central part of the state.
- **Dinosaur National Monument:** A site where fossils from the Jurassic period are found.
- **Bear Lake:** Known as the "Caribbean of the Rockies" due to its unique turquoise-blue color.
- **Golden Spike:** Celebrates the completion of the first Transcontinental Railroad.

Vermont

- **Green Mountain State:** The nickname comes from the French "Vert Mont," or "Green Mountain."
- **Maple Syrup:** Vermont is the largest producer of maple syrup in the United States.
- **Ben & Jerry's:** The popular ice cream company started in Burlington, Vermont, in 1978.
- **Montpelier:** The smallest state capital in the U.S., and the only one without a McDonald's.
- **Vermont Republic:** Before becoming a state, Vermont was an independent republic from 1777 to 1791.
- **Calvin Coolidge:** The 30th President of the U.S., born in Plymouth, Vermont.
- **Lake Champlain:** The sixth-largest body of fresh water in the U.S., forming part of the border with New York.
- **Ski Resorts:** Vermont has over 20 alpine ski resorts and is a popular winter destination.
- **Marble Quarrying:** Vermont is the leading U.S. producer of slate and the second largest producer of marble.
- **Green Mountain National Forest:** The largest National Forest in the state, covering 399,151 acres.
- **Vermont Teddy Bear Company:** One of the largest producers of teddy bears in the U.S.
- **Vermont's Constitution:** The first to prohibit slavery.
- **Morgan Horse:** The official state animal, and one of the earliest horse breeds developed in the United States.
- **Cheese Production:** Vermont produces over 150 varieties of cheese.
- **Appalachian Trail:** A portion of the famous 2,200-mile hiking trail crosses through Vermont.
- **Camels Hump:** One of Vermont's most recognized mountains due to its distinctive, camel-like profile.

- **Dairy Farming:** Vermont has the highest number of dairy farms per capita in the U.S.
- **The Long Trail:** The oldest long-distance hiking trail in the U.S., running the length of Vermont.
- **Norwich University:** The first private military college in the U.S., founded in 1819.
- **Mad River Glen:** The ski area with the last operating single-chair lift in the U.S.

Virginia

- **Mother of Presidents:** Virginia is the birthplace of eight U.S. Presidents, more than any other state.
- **Jamestown:** The first permanent English settlement in the Americas, established in 1607.
- **Arlington National Cemetery:** The final resting place for over 400,000 military veterans and their dependents.
- **Pentagon:** The world's largest office building is located in Arlington, Virginia.
- **Williamsburg:** Colonial Williamsburg is a living-history museum portraying colonial American life in the 18th century.
- **CIA Headquarters:** Located in Langley, Virginia.
- **Virginia Tech:** One of the top research universities in the U.S., located in Blacksburg.
- **Appalachian Trail:** A substantial part of this 2,200-mile trail runs through Virginia.
- **Shenandoah National Park:** Known for its stunning vistas along the Skyline Drive.
- **Navy's Birthplace:** The U.S. Navy was born in Virginia in 1775.
- **Peanuts:** Virginia is known for its gourmet peanuts, particularly the super-large Virginia-type peanuts.
- **Hampton Roads:** One of the world's largest natural harbors located at the mouth of the Chesapeake Bay.
- **Virginia State Capitol:** The first state capitol building to be modeled after a Roman temple.
- **Mount Vernon:** George Washington's plantation home, located along the Potomac River.
- **Virginia Beach:** The longest pleasure beach in the world.
- **Blue Ridge Mountains:** Known for their bluish color when seen from a distance.
- **Internet Traffic:** An estimated 70% of the world's Internet traffic passes through data centers in Loudoun County.

- **Barboursville Ruins:** The only building in the U.S. designed by Thomas Jefferson for a friend that has been preserved as a ruin.
- **Smithfield Ham:** Genuine Smithfield hams, which must be cured within the town limits of Smithfield, are a Virginia specialty.
- **NASA Langley Research Center:** The first field center for NASA, located in Hampton.

Washington

- **Evergreen State:** Washington's nickname stems from its lush evergreen forests.
- **Seattle:** The birthplace of grunge music and Starbucks, is the largest city in the state.
- **Mount Rainier:** This active stratovolcano is the highest mountain in the state.
- **Space Needle:** An iconic observation tower in Seattle, built for the 1962 World's Fair.
- **Boeing:** The world's largest aerospace company was founded in Seattle.
- **Apple Production:** Washington State produces more apples than any other state.
- **Olympic National Park:** The park is known for its diversity with the Pacific coastline, alpine areas, and rainforests.
- **Pike Place Market:** One of the oldest continuously operated public farmers' markets in the United States.
- **Microsoft Corporation:** This tech giant, co-founded by Bill Gates, has its headquarters in Redmond.
- **Grand Coulee Dam:** The largest concrete structure and the largest electricity-producing facility in the United States.
- **Amazon Headquarters:** Amazon, the multinational technology company, is headquartered in Seattle.
- **Puget Sound:** A complex of estuarine water bodies famous for its beautiful scenery and marine life.
- **Spokane:** Known for being the birthplace of Father's Day.
- **Bainbridge Island:** Site of the first Japanese-American internment during World War II.
- **Hoh Rain Forest:** One of the largest temperate rainforests in the U.S.

- **Mount St. Helens:** Famous for its catastrophic 1980 eruption, the deadliest and most economically destructive volcanic event in U.S. history.
- **North Cascades National Park:** It has more glaciers than any other U.S. park outside Alaska.
- **Seattle Mariners:** Seattle's Major League Baseball team plays in T-Mobile Park.
- **San Juan Islands:** Known for whale watching, sea kayaking, and beautiful vistas.
- **Fort Vancouver:** A 19th-century fur trading post that was the headquarters of the Hudson's Bay Company.

West Virginia

- **Mountain State:** West Virginia is known as the Mountain State, with an average elevation of 1,500 feet, the highest of any U.S. state east of the Mississippi.
- **Harper's Ferry:** This historic town was the site of abolitionist John Brown's failed raid on the federal armory in 1859.
- **New River Gorge:** It's the longest and deepest river gorge in the Appalachian Mountains, famous for white-water rafting.
- **Coal Heritage:** West Virginia is the second-largest coal producing state in the U.S.
- **Mother's Day:** The first official Mother's Day observance took place in Grafton, West Virginia, in 1908.
- **West Virginia University:** One of the oldest public institutions in the state, founded in 1867.
- **The Greenbrier:** A luxury resort in White Sulphur Springs that served as a secret bunker to house Congress during the Cold War.
- **Hillbilly Hot Dogs:** A unique dining attraction famous for its enormous 15-inch Homewrecker hot dog.
- **Country Roads:** John Denver's song "Take Me Home, Country Roads" is one of the official state anthems.
- **Marbles Tournament:** The National Marbles Tournament has been held in West Virginia since 1922.
- **Golden Delicious:** The state fruit, first discovered in Clay County in the early 1900s.
- **Seneca Caverns:** One of the state's largest and most beautiful cavern systems, discovered by the Seneca Indians.
- **Hawks Nest State Park:** Known for its panoramic views of the New River Gorge.
- **Blackwater Falls:** A five-story waterfall and one of the state's most photographed sights.
- **Trans-Allegheny Lunatic Asylum:** One of the largest hand-cut stone masonry buildings in America, it's reportedly haunted.

- **Kanawha State Forest:** Known for its diverse wildflower and bird populations.
- **Cass Scenic Railroad:** Provides a glimpse into the state's logging history with rides on original steam-driven locomotives.
- **Mothman:** A legendary creature reportedly seen in the Point Pleasant area during the 1960s.
- **Charleston:** The state capital and largest city in West Virginia.
- **Monongahela National Forest:** The forest contains more than 900,000 acres of land, making it the third-largest national forest east of the Rockies.

Wisconsin

- **Dairyland:** Wisconsin is famously known as the Dairy Capital of the United States, producing more dairy products, particularly cheese, than any other state.
- **Harley-Davidson:** The iconic motorcycle manufacturer was founded in Milwaukee, Wisconsin in 1903.
- **Forward State:** Wisconsin's motto, symbolizing its continuous drive to be a national leader.
- **Ice Age Trail:** One of only eleven National Scenic Trails in the U.S., it highlights the state's unique glacial features.
- **Waterpark Capital:** Wisconsin Dells is recognized as the "Waterpark Capital of the World," boasting the highest concentration of water parks on the globe.
- **Ringling Brothers:** The famous Ringling Brothers circus was founded in Baraboo, Wisconsin in 1884.
- **Green Bay Packers:** The only non-profit, community-owned major league professional sports team in the U.S.
- **Bratwurst Tradition:** Wisconsin is known for its bratwursts, even hosting the annual Bratwurst Days festival.
- **State Capitol:** The state's capitol building in Madison is the only one built of granite.
- **State Parks:** Wisconsin boasts 47 fun-filled state parks, 13 state forests, and many other recreational areas.
- **The House on the Rock:** An eccentric tourist attraction featuring a distinct complex of architecturally unique rooms, streets, gardens, and shops.
- **EAA AirVenture Show:** An annual gathering of aviation enthusiasts in Oshkosh, it's the largest of its kind in the world.
- **Leinenkugel's:** A well-known beer brewed in Chippewa Falls, Wisconsin since 1867.
- **American Birkebeiner:** The largest cross-country ski race in North America is held in Hayward, Wisconsin.

- **Art's Fishing Shop:** Open since 1936, it's the world's largest musky shop located in Minocqua.
- **Cheeseheads:** A fun nickname for Wisconsin citizens, derived from the state's association with cheese.
- **Door County:** Known for its cherry orchards and the 300 miles of picturesque shoreline.
- **Milk Production:** Wisconsin is second only to California in terms of milk production.
- **Wisconsin River:** The state's longest river, it stretches over 430 miles from its source near the Michigan border to its mouth on the Mississippi River.
- **Milwaukee Art Museum:** Its stunning building features a moveable sunscreen with a 217-foot wingspan.

Wyoming

- **Yellowstone:** The first National Park in the U.S. and in the world was established in Wyoming in 1872.
- **Equality State:** Wyoming's nickname, reflecting its status as the first state to grant women the right to vote in 1869.
- **Old Faithful:** The famous geyser located in Yellowstone National Park is one of the most predictable geothermal features on Earth.
- **Devils Tower:** America's first National Monument, established in 1906, features a striking geological feature that rises dramatically from the surrounding plains.
- **Buffalo Bill Center of the West:** This center in Cody, Wyoming consists of five museums and a research library dedicated to the American West.
- **Wind River Range:** Home to more than 40 peaks over 13,000 feet, including Gannett Peak, the highest point in Wyoming.
- **Least Populated:** Despite being the 10th largest by area, Wyoming is the least populated state in the U.S.
- **The Jackalope:** A mythical rabbit-like creature with antelope horns, often associated with the state.
- **Hot Springs State Park:** The park in Thermopolis features the world's largest mineral hot spring.
- **Grand Teton National Park:** Known for its stunning mountain landscapes, abundant wildlife, and pristine lakes.
- **Rodeo Capital:** Cheyenne is known as the Rodeo Capital of the World and hosts the largest outdoor rodeo, Cheyenne Frontier Days.
- **Cattle Industry:** Wyoming's economy has been heavily dependent on cattle ranching since the late 19th century.
- **Flaming Gorge:** A popular outdoor recreation area featuring a large reservoir and dramatic cliffs.
- **J.C. Penney Stores:** The first store of this national retail chain was opened in Kemmerer, Wyoming in 1902.

- **Trona Industry:** Wyoming is one of the world's top producers of trona, a mineral used to make soda ash.
- **Wild Horses:** Wyoming is home to more wild horses than any other state in the U.S.
- **Coal Production:** Wyoming leads the U.S. in coal production, accounting for about 40% of the nation's total.
- **Snowmobiling:** Wyoming has over 2,000 miles of groomed and ungroomed public snowmobile trails.
- **Indian Paintbrush:** Wyoming's state flower, a colorful species of wildflower found in many parts of the state.
- **Bighorn River:** Known as a premier location for fly fishing, particularly for trout.

Conclusion

And so, we conclude the first volume of our series, "1000 Facts about The United States of America". As we reach the end of this thrilling exploration, we hope that these first 1000 facts have served not just as tidbits of trivia, but as windows into the vibrant tapestry of American life, history, and culture.

From the natural grandeur of national parks to the resonating echoes of historical events, the cultural nuances of unique regions to remarkable scientific breakthroughs, the United States presents itself as a captivating array of diverse stories. Each state, each fact, each anecdote offers a piece of this larger picture, constructing a vivid narrative that illuminates the country's past and hints at its future.

While we've reached the end of this volume, remember this is merely the first step on a much larger journey. There are 2000 more facts awaiting your discovery in the subsequent volumes, each one as intriguing and enlightening as the last. As we close this book, we invite you to continue this exploration, to keep the spirit of curiosity alive, and to delve even deeper into the fascinating saga of the United States in our upcoming volumes.

Thank you for joining us in unraveling the wonders of this great nation. Here's to the beginning of a remarkable journey, and the promise of even more to come.

Daniel Scott